1

Author Information

Candy Praise, also referred to as Evangelist Candy, is a multi-gifted woman of God who embodies a rich array of talents. In this compelling autobiography, she orates a fascinating, courageous and brave account of the stark reality of being a survivor.

Bad things happen to good people but good people also happen to bad things. When He met her in a wretched state, she writes, my testimony is that it's because of His goodness that I am Fully Alive today. He is a good God. My voice, that's always celebrated, has been preserved so that He can speak and sing through me to the most devastated souls in the earth and bring His power and light for the radical transformation of others.

What looked like a hopeless case scenario has been the backdrop to the miraculous journey Candy has had throughout her life so far. Good things do come out opposing experiences after all. With God being her keeper from dangers seen and unseen, she narrates that every trap set before her was set up for her to become a statistic, but she is a living witness of the tangible miracle that she is and ultimately owes this all to her Heavenly Father.

This book was written in part to inspire other survivors and those who have a heart for such souls to see that God creates beauty from ashes. He turns pain into purpose and battles into blessings and a glorious light awaits those who choose to win to champion others as they do.

Copyright

Dedication

I dedicate this book To The Lord Jesus Christ whom without His power and strength that is mighty to save I would not be alive. This book has been in the making for over eight years, I recognise that now more than ever my life is a living "miracle". It's because of God's amazing grace that I have been able to chronicle my experience in the hope that it will encourage someone not to give up and empower the hopeless. I think this is one of the bravest things I have ever done.

There is not enough space here to thank God for giving me the grace to write my story. I am eternally filled with gratitude, He has been my everything and has kept me when I couldn't keep myself. By His grace, I found the determination to write my narrative. There are a group of people who I know will be blessed and encouraged by how God has enabled me to overcome.

There are so so many people to thank but in particular, I want to thank Corby and Chryso and to the many servants of God, too many to name, who have ministered His grace to me in immeasurable ways. To my beloved friends thank you for your unwavering support and encouragement and to many other special people that are too many to mention here but you know who you are. May God bless you all so richly and may He prosper you thousand times more. Amen

Prologue

Bad things happen to good people but good people also happen to bad things. He met me in a wretched state, my testimony is that it's because of His goodness I am fully alive today. He is a keeper and a good God.

My voice, that's always been celebrated, has been preserved so that He can speak and sing through me. To speak to the most devastated souls on the Earth and bring His power and light for the radical transformation of others.

Maybe, I can celebrate the glory of the Lord here with a special song in my heart. Could it have been part of His master plan for me to experience so much devastation, family breakdown, loss and abandonment as an infant so that He could ultimately be glorified?

What looked like a hopeless scenario has been the backdrop to the miraculous journey I have experienced in my life so far. Good things do come out of Nazareth, after all. He is always being glorified as my heavenly Father. Every trap set before me was setting me up to become a statistic, but I am a living witness that Jesus Is Alive.

Being a former child of the state-led me to have a revelation that it was "He" that "Raised Me Up", as the song so rightly says.

Maybe I should have called this book "Songs". After all, God is a singer which is why I love the scripture that says, "The Lord thy God in the midst of thee is mighty; he will save, he will rejoice over thee with joy; he will rest in his love, he will joy over thee with singing" (Zephaniah 3:17)

The song "You Raised My Up" by Josh Groban is my personal testimony. Have a listen to my rendition on my YouTube channel @ Candy Praise. He writes

When I am down, and, oh, my soul, so weary
When troubles come, and my heart burdened be
Then, I am still and wait here in the silence
Until you come and sit awhile with me
You raise me up, so I can stand on mountains
You raise me up to walk on stormy seas
I am strong when I am on your shoulders
You raise me up to more than I can be

Recently I went on a training day for children's mental health first aid. I am passionate about the younger generation, particularly those that have been in care, otherwise known as "Looked After" children. Having worked as a residential social worker in the early 1990s, and later becoming a sociologist and lecturer in further education, I have been really keen to empower them.

With youth crime on the rise, among a plethora of other issues facing the next generation, I wanted to equip myself with some practical tools that I could use with the group that I am most passionate about empowering.

I was confronted with over twenty-five barriers that children are challenged with. Especially children like me who were children of the state. It nearly winded me. I was confronted with the reality again, as to the mammoth mountains that all so often challenged me and made me want to give up and die. These obstacles were intimidating, daunting, cruel and scary and often made me weep.

The barriers reminded me of what caused me to become a fighter. Fighting for my right to be treated with love, dignity, and respect, to stay alive. It has not been easy. It's great to have these resilient qualities but it is by no means a walk in the park. In fact, the complete opposite. Often it's been gruelling, at other times, it has been exciting to see what God has done in my life. Sometimes I have been stunned to experience the miracle that God has made me to be.

Many people I meet and engage with say things like, I love your energy, your presence is radiant and bright or you are so colourful. Many say I am like sunshine, that when I walk in the room it lights up. This I know to be the presence of God. At my core, I am a beautiful and loving child of God. It makes my heart so glad that I get to shine the light and love of God onto some of the most hurting souls and enable them to experience His amazing grace.

Being an ex-care leaver too, I am mindful that I am a role model to young people, which is what I needed when I was their age. I needed somebody that I could relate to from the older generation, to glean wisdom from but sadly it was non-existent. Instead, I read autobiographies by Maya Angelou, who herself was a survivor of childhood abuse & other stories alike. Individuals like this were real lifelines for me, to inspire me to learn life skills and ways to cope with the overwhelming social, emotional, economical, spiritual, maternal and paternal deprivation and the stigmatisation that comes with being labelled as a child of the state.

I have chosen to become what I needed when I was a child. An encourager, comforter, hope giver. To be a source of empowerment and inspiration- and as the song says. This little light of mine, I'm gonna let it shine.

On reflection, I wonder though if these barriers from that day on the mental health first aid training, was God's way of giving me my gifts? There was a champion in me that was being built up to overcome through facing obstacle after obstacle and fighting lions and bears. God was giving me the gift of deep empathy in order to equip me to be sensitive to the suffering of others, to offer encouragement to the soul that was weathered and tired of holding on. These multiple obstacles were preparing me to become an emboldened woman of God to empty hell and fill heaven, to rise up with boldness and power and bring the intense love of God to the hardest of hearts. To be the evangelist that I am!

What had I endured and overcome, was this somehow meant to give me a unique humility? Was it this grace given to me that made people approach me all the time, some even wanting what I had, the Jesus in me?

I do think that reframing what we go through can be done in a way, not only to empower oneself but ultimately uplift and empower others. I mean, every great person I know became great because of the challenges that they have overcome. Jesus Christ suffered the cruellest of deaths, His assassination was the ultimate love offering. His life was sacrificed so that I could live.

There are NO WORDS for what He has done for me.

I AM A LIVING MIRACLE. This song is a testament to the love that my Heavenly Father has poured out into my heart.

Amazing Grace
Amazing Grace, how sweet the sound
That saved a wretch like me
I once was lost, but now am found
Was blind but now I see

Was Grace that taught my heart to fear

And Grace, my fears relieved

How precious did that Grace appear

The hour I first believed

Through many dangers, toils and snares

We have already come

T'was Grace that brought us safe thus far

And Grace will lead us home

The following scriptures are of huge encouragement to me.

He said, "if I am lifted up I will draw all men unto me". (John 12:32)

When I was down, He was up to something, when I was being rejected my faith was being perfected, when I didn't think I was going to make it in the midnight hour

He graced me with new mercies every morning, and great is thy faithfulness.

Lamentations 3:22-23(ESV), "The steadfast love of the Lord never ceases; His mercies never come to an end; They are new every morning, great is your faithfulness".

Psalm 24:7-10 "Lift up your heads, O ye gates; and be ye lift up, ye everlasting doors; and the King of glory shall come in.8 Who is this King of glory? The Lord strong and mighty, the Lord mighty in battle.9 Lift up your heads, O ye gates; even lift them up, ye everlasting doors; and the King of glory shall come in.0 Who is this King of glory? The Lord of hosts, he is the King of glory. Selah".

He made a way for me in what looked like a hopeless situation His glory was revealed here and made a way as the song says,

Waymaker

You are here

Moving in our midst

I worship you

I worship you

You are here

Working in this place

I worship you

I worship you

You are here

Moving in our midst

I worship you

I worship you

You are here

Working in this place

I worship you

I worship you

Way maker

Miracle worker

Promise keeper

Light in the darkness

My God

That is who you are

Way maker

Miracle worker

Promise keeper

Light in the darkness

My God

That is who you are

Songwriter Sinach

My survival is a testament that He is alive today and He has risen. I am a living miracle because it is no longer I that lives but Christ who lives in me Galatians 2:20

He turned my scars into stars and gave me a purpose for my pain. That purpose is to use the voice He has given me to worship, build up, encourage, edify, evangelise. To be a voice for the voiceless, and be a mother in zion for deprived and abandoned children. I know I will be with my children in The Lord soon.Isaiah 54:17. By faith, it is so. He spared my life so that I could reach out to others and minister His comfort and love.

I will always give praise unto Him because He has been and is the keeper of my soul.

A few words from an amazing song that comes to mind, " If you've got pain, He's a pain taker".

It is my hope that as you read about my story that you will be able to see the hand of God in my life. Maybe, you will be encouraged to see how He is the good that can change ashes into beauty.

Isaiah 61:33, "To appoint unto them that mourn in Zion, to give unto them beauty for ashes, the oil of joy for mourning, the garment of praise for the spirit of heaviness; that they might be called trees of righteousness, the planting of the Lord, that he might be glorified".

You now have an idea of where God has brought me from and where He has taken me to. I hope you will see His victorious hand at work in my life. The pain I have endured has not been for myself, but for lost, dying and hurt people who are desperate for a lifeline and in need of a miracle. The reason why I am passionate about encouraging others and winning souls is because when salvation came in 1997 and I received The Lord, Christ changed my life.

What a joy it is, such an honour to share the love of Christ in my heart. God continues to restore me as I stand on (Joel 2:25).

Psalms 51 says in verse five that I was born in sin and this particular scripture is etched on my heart because of the work of the cross. It's my daily prayer of repentance as I continue to appreciate what He did at Golgatha for me and the remission of my sins. I know for sure that without the gift of salvation, and the healing Christ has bestowed upon me and for my transgressions, that, I would not be alive to testify of His goodness and preservation of my life.

Psalms 51

1 Have mercy upon me, O God, according to thy lovingkindness: according to the multitude of thy tender mercies blot out my transgressions.2 Wash me thoroughly from mine iniquity, and cleanse me from my

sin.3 For I acknowledge my transgressions: and my sin is ever before me.4 Against thee, thee only, have I sinned, and done this evil in thy sight: that thou mightiest be justified when thou speakest and be clear when thou judgest.5 Behold, I was shaped in iniquity, and in sin did my mother conceive me.6 Behold, thou desire truth in the inward parts: and in the hidden part thou shalt make me know wisdom.7 Purge me with hyssop, and I shall be clean: wash me, and I shall be whiter than snow.8 Make me hear joy and gladness; that the bones which thou hast broken may rejoice.9 Hide thy face from my sins, and blot out all mine iniquities.10 Create in me a clean heart, O God; and renew a right spirit within me.11 Cast me not away from thy presence, and take not thy holy spirit from me.12 Restore unto me the joy of thy salvation; uphold me with thy free spirit.13 Then will I teach transgressors thy ways; and sinners shall be converted unto thee.14 Deliver me from blood guiltiness, O God, thou God of my salvation: and my tongue shall sing aloud of thy righteousness.15 O Lord, open thou my lips; and my mouth shall shew forth thy praise.16 For thou desire not sacrifice; else would I give it: thou delightest not in burnt offering.17 The sacrifices of God are a broken spirit: a broken and a contrite heart, O God, thou wilt not despise.18 Do good in thy good pleasure unto Zion: build thou the walls of Jerusalem.19 Then shalt thou be pleased with the sacrifices of righteousness, with burnt offering and whole burnt offering: then shall they offer bullocks upon thine altar.

Ultimately God purchased my freedom, "the thief cometh not, but for to steal, and to kill, and to destroy: I have come that they might have life and that they might have it more abundantly". John 10:10

Despite the challenges that life presented, God has blessed me with abundance.. I am not my circumstances. I am who God says I am, as the scripture says, "but we have this treasure in earthen vessels that the Excellency of the power may be of God, and not of us". 2 Corinthians 4:7

I understand there's a challenge that as I speak from experience and chronicle my story, there can be a massive discrepancy between faith and reality. The sovereign word, although the absolute truth can be the complete opposite to your circumstances. We are children of faith, and as His beloved children he requires us to "walk by faith and not by sight" 2 Corinthians 5:7

By using my faith I chose not to repeat negative generational cycles in my life. I chose to become a multi award scholar and became a sociologist at thirty years old.

Below are some of the scriptures that are my go to's which enable me to live victoriously.

'By His stripes you are healed". 1 Peter 2:24.

Now faith is the substance of things hoped for, the evidence of things not seen. Hebrews 11:1

But without faith, it is impossible to please him: for him that cometh to God must believe that he is and that he is a rewarder of them that diligently seek him. Hebrews 11:6

I am a work in progress, truth be told I could have ended up in complete destitution if it was not for His abounding love. I could have ended up dead, buried, homeless, on drugs, the list goes on. HE SAVED ME FROM DEATH AND DESTRUCTION.

To the praise of the glory of his grace, wherein he hath made us accepted in the beloved. Ephesians 1:6

It's my prayer for you that as I take you on this journey of my life story, that through the anguish, tears that the presence of the Lord will empower and comfort you. I hope you will see that He is faithful, that He is real, alive and that just as He has been with me throughout that you will be reassured that He is with you too.

Thankfully I can testify that I have overcome by the blood of the lamb and the word of my testimony. Revelation 12:11 King James Version

I hear some people ask "If there is a God, then why is there so much hurt and suffering?" I have to confess that in some of my darkest moments, I couldn't fathom why either.

I've cried out like this, even into adulthood. I've lost count of the number of times I've said "all I've done is come into the world and born into this, I didn't ask to come here and experience such tragedy!".

God is so faithful and he began to reveal key things to me. The Lord taught me about generational iniquity, that I had to repent for some of the sins of my forefathers, which created open doors for the enemy to come in. God then revealed to me the blessing of Holy Matrimony and the significance of being in a God-ordained marriage that is a blessing. I wasn't carried through marriage which created a door for the enemy to come in. He showed me the power of names, that your name is attached to your destiny. So I believe the enemy saw that and thought there's no way I'm gonna let her walk in her nobility and authority and rule and reign with dominion and power.

He showed me that my biological family knew no better. I initially lived in a large extended family, but my grandparents main concern was with working, putting food on the table, and paying the bills.

Christ became a curse for me. When He went on the cross He bore my sins, all of them. He redeemed me from the curse of the law by becoming a curse for me, for it is written: "Cursed is everyone who hangs on a tree. "Galatians 3:13 KJV

He has been my everything. Literally, Jesus, the messiah, has been a very present help in times of trouble.

Psalms 46:1

I am constantly forgiving because of who He is. In all honesty, writing my story has been paradoxical. On the one hand it's been healing but some pretty serious unhealed wounds were revisited and as painful as it was these hurts needed to come to the surface so that I could learn to acknowledge the truth, release and give it all to God. He told me to cast all my cares on Him because He cares for me.

1 Peter 5:7, again though, it's ongoing and thanks be to God I can come to him any time and approach the throne of His grace with boldness.

I have experienced such an outpouring of His amazing love that I find myself wanting to write with the pen of praise. Actually, more like write Him a love song so that I can worship Him for who He is. Jesus..........Glory to your name......You are the lifter of my head. If it was not for you, Oh God, where would I be Lord?

At the same time all the trauma and loss I have survived, resurrecting these painful memories has not been easy. He said, "let the weak say that they are strong." It is because of His mercies I am not consumed.

That is why, for Christ's sake, I delight in weaknesses, in insults, in hardships, in persecutions, in difficulties. For when I am weak, then I am strong. 2 Corinthians 12:10.

I am the first woman in my family whose complete support system is God. Salvation had to start somewhere and it started with me in 1997. I've literally been stripped back to Him and Him alone.

It's so comforting to know that He preserves me and protects me as promised in Psalms 91. The Lord said that He's going to work on me and use my suffering as a living testimony to the nations. The blessing in all of this is that He is doing such great work in my life! This is why my story has been so poignant for me to scribe.

It's interesting how some negative generational cycles have not been repeated in the family bloodline. Alcohol abuse stopped with me, a generational pattern that has been rife. I'm the first in my family to become a multi-award-winning scholar and professional. I'm the first woman to have mobilised through the class system and become a sociologist lecturer, trainer, biblical life coach, mentor, artist, singer, songwriter, poet, author and orator. I have emerged from extremely humble beginnings and adverse and complex deprivation.

I was the first female to begin driving at a very young age. For me, that was a huge achievement, this was just not the norm in the family that I was born into. The day I passed my test I was on the ultimate natural high. I felt like a WINNER!

Another major triumph is that I don't define myself from my past in any way, shape, or form. While some of these things seem quite reasonable to me, this is a vast triumph of rising above the statistics of children who suffer maternal and paternal deprivation, and are subject to abuse as a child of the state. Jesus has indeed made a way where there seemed to be no way.

Christ redeemed me from the curse of the law by becoming a curse for me, for it is written: "Cursed is everyone who is hung on a pole. Galatians 3:13 I thank God for so many triumphs. See the chapter of signs and wonders.

I was a disadvantaged child that was denied the right to family life, denied loving relationships with my caregivers and abandoned. But it's the grace of God that has kept me alive and victorious. He has been merciful to me. I am triumphant because of Him.

According to the statistics, survivors of the care system without a family, don't do that well. Mortality rates are high and the effects of gross deprivation and adversity are often correlated to criminality and chronic health conditions to name but a few.

Low self-esteem and poor confidence can impact quite heavily on education which in turn can negatively influence work prospects, affecting the overall quality of life. Can you see the potential downward spiral? I had all the odds stacked against me, BUT GOD. I am victorious, triumphant, and winning and continue to excel in all areas of my life, because Christ has redeemed me from the curse of the law. Galatians 3:13

You intended to harm me, but God intended it for good to accomplish what is now being done, the saving of many lives (Genesis 50:20 NIV)

I pray that as you read my story you will also see the hand of God at work as I have experience writing about my life. In essence, It's my heart's cry that you will encounter the true and living God, the one who loves us with an everlasting love.

I pray that like me, a message will come out of your mess and minister to you. That your purpose may be manifested through your pain. That triumph will come out of your tragedy and hope will be birthed out of your hurt. He is able. I am a living witness

He wanted me to write my story because He showed me a dying people needing to be saved from perishing and the urgency for their redemption. It is not His will that any should perish. I have a powerful calling on my life as an evangelist and you may even sense my passion to love on the needy, oppressed and lost and to win souls and populate heaven.

For God so loved the world, that he gave his only begotten Son, that whosoever believeth in him should not perish, but have everlasting life. John 3:16 KJV

THE LORD HAS MADE ME TO BE A LIVING STONE! An Epistle! A mystery. I AM A MIRACLE.

The below passages are some of the promises that Abba Father has blessed me to receive which are God breathed and sustaining my life.

For our present troubles are quite small and won't last very long. Yet they produce for us an immeasurably great glory that will last forever! 2 Corinthians 4:17 NLT

Psalm 118:22 ASV The stone which the builders rejected has become the chief cornerstone

Psalms 30:5 Weeping may endure for a night, but joy cometh in the morning.

Psalm 126 When the Lord turned again the captivity of Zion, we were like them that dream.

Romans 8 And we know that in all things God works for the good of those who love him, who[a] have been called according to his purpose.

1 Peter 2:9 But you are not like that, for you have been chosen by God himself—you are priests of the King, you are holy and pure, you are God's very own—all this so that you may show to others how God called you out of the darkness into his wonderful light. Living Translation.

Why Grounding?

I have included this section on grounding as some of the issues my story raises are quite sensitive. I felt that it was necessary to offer some techniques to use, should you read something that is triggering. By using some of these grounding techniques, it can help to regulate your emotional state and prioritise your emotional wellbeing. I practice wellbeing myself including massage, aromatherapy and singing which induce a peaceful and calming state.

It's also a practice that can help you pull away from flashbacks, unwanted memories, and negative or challenging emotions.

These techniques may help distract you from what you're experiencing and refocus on what's happening in the present moment.

You can use grounding techniques to help create space from distressing feelings in nearly any situation, but they're especially helpful if you're dealing with

- anxiety
- post-traumatic stress disorder
- dissociation
- traumatic memories

- substance use disorder

Physical techniques

These techniques use your five senses or tangible objects — things you can touch — to help you move through distress.

1. Pick up or touch items near you

Are the things you touch soft or hard? Heavy or light? Warm or cool? Focus on the texture and colour of each item. Challenge yourself to think of specific colours, such as crimson, burgundy, indigo, or turquoise, instead of simply red or blue.

2.Breathe deeply

Slowly inhale, then exhale. If it helps, you can say or think "in" and "out" with each breath. Feel each breath filling your lungs and note how it feels to push it back out.

3.Savor a food or drink

Take small bites or sips of a food or beverage you enjoy, letting yourself fully taste each bite. Think about how it tastes and smells and the flavours that linger on your tongue.

4. Take a short walk

Concentrate on your steps — you can even count them. Notice the rhythm of your footsteps and how it feels to put your foot on the ground and then lift it again.

5. Hold a piece of ice

What does it feel like at first? How long does it take to start melting? How does the sensation change when the ice begins to melt?

6.Savor a scent

Is there a fragrance that appeals to you? This might be a cup of tea, an herb or spice, a favourite soap, or a scented candle. Inhale the fragrance slowly and deeply and try to note its qualities (sweet, spicy, sharp, citrusy, and so on).

7. Move your body

Do a few exercises or stretches. You could try jumping jacks, jumping up and down, jumping rope, jogging in place, or stretching different muscle groups one by one.

Pay attention to how your body feels with each movement and when your hands or feet touch the floor or move through the air. How does the floor feel against your feet and hands? If you jump rope, listen to the sound of the rope in the air and when it hits the ground.

8. Listen to your surroundings

Take a few moments to listen to the noises around you. Do you hear birds? Dogs barking? Machinery or traffic? If you hear people talking, what are they saying? Do you recognize the language? Let the sounds wash over you and remind you where you are.

9.Feel your body

You can do this sitting or standing. Focus on how your body feels from head to toe, noticing each part.

Can you feel your hair on your shoulders or forehead? Glasses on your ears or nose? The weight of your shirt on your shoulders? Do your arms feel loose or stiff at your sides? Can you feel your heartbeat? Is it rapid or steady? Does your stomach feel full, or are you hungry? Are your legs crossed, or are your feet resting on the floor? Is your back straight?

Curl your fingers and wiggle your toes. Are you barefoot or in shoes? How does the floor feel against your feet?

Mental techniques

These grounding exercises use mental distractions to help redirect your thoughts away from distressing feelings and back to the present.

1. Play a memory game

Look at a detailed photograph or picture (like a cityscape or other "busy" scene) for 5 to 10 seconds. Then, turn the photograph face-down and recreate the photograph in your mind, in as much detail as possible. Or, you can mentally list all the things you remember from the picture.

2 Think in categories

Choose one or two broad categories, such as "musical instruments," "ice cream flavours," "mammals," or "baseball teams." Take a minute or two to mentally list as many things from each category as you can.

3. Use maths and numbers

Even if you aren't a maths person, numbers can help centre you.

Try:

- running through a times table in your head.
- counting backward from 100
- choosing a number and thinking of five ways you could make the number ($6 + 11 = 17$, $20 - 3 = 17$, $8 \times 2 + 1 = 17$, etc.)

4. Recite something

Think of a poem, song, or book passage you know by heart. Recite it quietly to yourself or in your head. If you say the words aloud, focus on the shape of each word on your lips and in your mouth. If you say the words in your head, visualise each word as you'd see it on a page.

5. Make yourself laugh

Make up a silly joke — the kind you'd find on a candy wrapper or popsicle stick.

You might also make yourself laugh by watching your favourite funny animal video, a clip from a comedian or TV show you enjoy, or anything else you know will make you laugh.

6. Visualise a daily task you enjoy or don't mind doing

If you like doing laundry, for example, think about how you'd put away a finished load.

"The clothes feel warm coming out of the dryer. They're soft and a little stiff at the same time. They feel light in the basket, even though they spill over the top. I'm spreading them out over the bed so they won't wrinkle. I'm folding the towels first, shaking them out before folding them into halves, then thirds," and so on.

7. Describe a common task

Think of an activity you do often or can do very well, such as making coffee, locking up your office, or tuning a guitar. Go through the process step-by-step, as if you're giving someone else instructions on how to do it.

8.Imagine yourself leaving the painful feelings behind

Picture yourself:

- gathering the emotions, balling them up, and putting them into a box

- walking, swimming, biking, or jogging away from painful feelings
- imagining your thoughts as a song or TV show you dislike, changing the channel or turning down the volume — they're still there, but you don't have to listen to them.

9. Describe what's around you

Spend a few minutes taking in your surroundings and noting what you see. Use all five senses to provide as much detail as possible. "This bench is red, but the bench over there is green. It's warm under my jeans since I'm sitting in the sun. It feels rough, but there aren't any splinters. The grass is yellow and dry. The air smells like smoke. I hear kids having fun and two dogs barking."

Soothing techniques

You can use these techniques to comfort yourself in times of emotional distress. These exercises can help promote good feelings that may help the negative feelings fade or seem less overwhelming.

1.Picture the voice or face of someone you love

If you feel upset or distressed, visualise someone positive in your life. Imagine their face or think of what their voice sounds like. Imagine them telling you that the moment is tough, but that you'll get through it.

2.Practice self-kindness

Repeat kind, compassionate phrases to yourself:

- "You're having a rough time, but you'll make it through."
- "You're strong, and you can move through this pain."
- "You're trying hard, and you're doing your best."

Say it, either aloud or in your head, as many times as you need

3. Sit with your pet

If you're at home and have a pet, spend a few moments just sitting with them. If they're of the furry variety, pet them, focusing on how their fur feels. Focus on their markings or unique characteristics. If you have a smaller pet you can hold, concentrate on how they feel in your hand.

Not at home? Think of your favourite things about your pet or how they would comfort you if they were there.

4. List favourites

List three favourite things in several different categories, such as foods, trees, songs, movies, books, places, and so on.

5. Visualise your favourite place

Think of your favourite place, whether it's the home of a loved one or a foreign country. Use all of your senses to create a mental image. Think of the colours you see, sounds you hear, and sensations you feel on your skin.

Remember the last time you were there. Who were you with, if anyone? What did you do there? How did you feel?

6. Plan an activity

This might be something you do alone or with a friend or loved one. Think of what you'll do and when. Maybe you'll go to dinner, take a walk on the beach, see a movie you've been looking forward to, or visit a museum.

Focus on the details, such as what you'll wear, when you'll go, and how you'll get there.

7. Touch something comforting

This could be your favourite blanket, a much-loved T-shirt, a smooth stone, a soft carpet, or anything that feels good to touch. Think about how it feels under your fingers or in your hand.

If you have a favourite sweater, scarf, or pair of socks, put them on and spend a moment thinking about the sensation of the fabric on your skin.

8. List positive things

Write or mentally list four or five things in your life that bring you joy, visualising each of them briefly.

9. I Listen to music

Put on your favourite song, but pretend you're listening to it for the first time. Focus on the melody and lyrics (if there are any). Does the song give you chills or create any other physical sensations? Pay attention to the parts that stand out most to you.

He Called Me Candy
Table of Contents

The Word, Worship & Warfare

I have been intentional about illustrating "every word from every song and passage here". It has been my lived experience of how the word of God which is sharper than any two-edged sword that continues to transform my life. This passage below is a perfect example.

Hebrews 4:12

For the word of God is quick, and powerful, and sharper than any two-edged sword, piercing even to the dividing asunder of soul and spirit, and of the joints and marrow, and is a discerner of the thoughts and intents of the heart

Words are so powerful and there's ginormous evidence to illustrate how words shape our reality. When I initially came across Dr Emoto's work I was fascinated to see how words take on a character from a scientific perspective. There is such a huge body of work on this, I could easily write a book about this as a stand-alone.

God's supreme and sovereign word though is so exceptional and so so powerful! I am a living witness and evidence that the word works. Below are just some passages that have continued to resonate and resound in my spirit.

Romans 10:17
So faith comes from hearing and hearing through the word of Christ
This passage is my total reality and I can honestly say that constantly listening, being built up and encouraged by listening to the true and living word continues to give me life.

Psalm 119:105

Your word is a lamp to my feet and a light to my path.

Just six months after I received salvation which you will read about later on, a precious sister in the Lord ministered this word to me during a testing time in my faith and I have to say it's become my living reality. He literally continues to light my path.

Psalms 119:105

Your word is a lamp to my feet, and a light to my path.

Jeremiah 15:16

Your words were found, and I ate them, and your words became to me a joy and the delight of my heart, for I am called by your name, O Lord, God of hosts.

So beautiful indeed that His word is the delight of my heart and the below scripture continuously reminds me of the faithfulness of what He has decreed.

Isaiah 55:11

So shall my word be that goes out from my mouth; it shall not return to me empty, but it shall accomplish that which I purpose, and shall succeed in the thing for which I sent it.

Amen & Amen that His word spoken over my life is established forever.

Matthew 4:4

But he answered, "It is written, "'Man shall not live by bread alone, but by every word that comes from the mouth of God.'"

Psalm 107:20

He sent out his word and healed them, and delivered them from their destruction.

Proverbs 18:21

Death and life are in the power of the tongue, and those who love it

John 1:1-51

In the beginning, was the Word, and the Word was with God, and the Word was God.

Genesis 1:3

And God said, "Let there be light," and there was light.

John 1:1-51

In the beginning was the Word, and the Word was with God, and the Word was God. He was in the beginning with God. All things were made through him, and without him was not any thing made that was made. In him was life, and the life was the light of men. The light shines in the darkness, and the darkness has not overcome it. ...

John 6:63

It is the Spirit who gives life; the flesh is no help at all. The words that I have spoken to you are spirit and life.

Hebrews 11:3

By faith we understand that the universe was created by the word of God, so that what is seen was not made out of things that are visible.

Colossians 3:16

Let the word of Christ dwell in you richly, teaching and admonishing one another in all wisdom, singing psalms and hymns and spiritual songs, with thankfulness in your hearts to God.

John 1:14

And the Word became flesh and dwelt among us, and we have seen his glory, glory as of the only Son from the Father, full of grace and truth.

Matthew 24:35

Heaven and earth will pass away, but my words will not pass away.

Every word sung and every scripture I've shared in my narrative was God's way of giving me the grace to write about my life. Especially during the final edit where waves of songs were coming hard and fast. His spirit was overwhelming me with joy that gave me supernatural strength.

Also, releasing the word through praise and worship has empowered me to wage a war against what was meant to destroy me. This for me has caused me to overcome and be triumphant.

Whenever I do sing, I am coming from a place of changing the atmosphere and fighting the good fight of faith. Also, singing for me is incredibly healing. It's a beautiful thing to enthrone God in praise and worship and bring heaven to earth. I know without a shadow of a doubt that when I have lifted up praises to God that he has been glorified and sustained me.

In 2013 when I wrote this, let's just say if I had the wisdom that I have acquired now, I may not have revisited my past in the relational and environmental context that I did. Of the many obstacles and hurdles life has thrown in my path without a shadow of a doubt this was one of "the most challenging". Sparing the details there is a passage that says in, Genesis 50:20 But as for you, you meant evil against me; but God meant it for good, in order to bring it about as it is today, to save many people's lives.

What was meant to destroy me, God is using for His good now. It is marvellous in His eyes. I would advise anyone with a traumatic past who wants to narrate their story to do so in a safe way. Maybe through a counsellor or therapist who is skilled and trained to work with survivors of abuse heal from multiple wounds in a safe way. I am encouraged that my scars have become stars so that I can shine His light into others in need. I am encouraged by the following passage.

Isaiah 61 1-7

1 The Spirit of the Lord God is upon me; because the Lord hath anointed me to preach good tidings unto the meek; he hath sent me to bind up the brokenhearted, to proclaim liberty to the captives, and the opening of the prison to them that are bound;

2 To proclaim the acceptable year of the Lord, and the day of vengeance of our God; to comfort all that mourn;

3 To appoint unto them that mourn in Zion, to give unto them beauty for ashes, the oil of joy for mourning, the garment of praise for the spirit of heaviness; that they might be called trees of righteousness, the planting of the Lord, that he might be glorified.

4 And they shall build the old wastes, they shall raise up the former desolations, and they shall repair the waste cities, the desolations of many generations.

5 And strangers shall stand and feed your flocks, and the sons of the alien shall be your plowmen and your vinedressers.

6 But ye shall be named the Priests of the Lord: men shall call you the Ministers of our God: ye shall eat the riches of the Gentiles, and in their glory shall ye boast yourselves.

7 For your shame ye shall have double; and for confusion they shall rejoice in their portion: therefore in their land they shall possess the double: everlasting joy shall be unto them.

The way my heavenly Father lavishes His love on me leaves me in awe. In this passage, His promises are that in Him I will be ablaze with glorious light and that He is giving me a delightful name. He goes so far as to say that I am a crown of glory and that He gives me a beautiful name, that I am a royal diadem in His hand. He said no more am I forsaken or left abandoned. That He delights in me. My response to this is "I'm Undone".

Isaiah 62

1 For Zion's sake will I not hold my peace, and for Jerusalem's sake I will not rest, until the righteousness thereof go forth as brightness, and the salvation thereof as a lamp that burneth.

2 And the Gentiles shall see thy righteousness, and all kings thy glory: and thou shalt be called by a new name, which the mouth of the Lord shall name.

3 Thou shalt also be a crown of glory in the hand of the Lord, and a royal diadem in the hand of thy God.

4 Thou shalt no more be termed Forsaken; neither shall thy land any more be termed Desolate: but thou shalt be called Hephzibah, and thy land Beulah: for the Lord delighteth in thee, and thy land shall be married.

A poignant song

Everlasting Good

Strength will rise as we wait upon the Lord

We will wait upon the Lord

We will wait upon the Lord

Strength will rise as we wait upon the Lord

We will wait upon the Lord

We will wait upon the Lord

Our God, You reign forever

Our hope, our strong deliverer

You are the everlasting God

The everlasting God

You do not faint

You won't grow weary

Strength will rise as we wait upon the Lord

We will wait upon the Lord

Writer(s): Brown Brenton Gifford, Riley Kenneth Henry

Singing the prayer of Jabez 1 Chronicles 4:10 because

"Jabez cried out to the God of Israel, "Oh that You would bless me and enlarge my territory! Let your hand be with me, and keep me from harm so that I will be free from pain." And God granted his request."

This song too has been liberating for me to sing as well.

No limits

No limits

No boundaries

I see increase

All around me

Stretch forth

Bring forth

I see increase

Enlarge my territory.

God wanted me to write my story not only for myself but as a declaration that as the scripture says in Revelation 12:11, "And they overcame him by the blood of the Lamb, and by the word of their testimony. I want this work to be a blessing for so many others. I pray for everyone, especially my biological family that God would bless them, each and everyone from the youngest to the eldest. I pray that He will overwhelm each one with His presence, with His light and with His love. That His perfect love would be tangible in their lives.

Not one of my family members has ever asked about my experiences growing up away from them. I have only just had this epiphany now while doing the last edit of this mammoth life work and just days away from publishing. It's been really liberating to share my narrative and bring to the light what was meant to destroy me that God has used it for His glory.

On that note, I am taken aback by some poignant passages, as illustrated from God delivered to me by one particular intercessor. As I was being showered by prayer these scriptures saturated me in a highly charged celestial atmosphere, the spirit rained down authority on me from heaven. I was immediately strengthened, empowered and fortified from Elohim. There I was standing in the midst of a severe prayer storm. Below were just some of the scriptures that girded me up and gave me power, strength and peace and so much more to help me in this process.

Luke 9:1

Then he called his twelve disciples together, and gave them power and authority over all devils, and to cure diseases.

Luke 10:19

Behold, I give unto you power to tread on serpents and scorpions, and over all the power of the enemy: and nothing shall by any means hurt you.

Genesis 6.3

And the LORD said, "My Spirit shall not strive with man forever, for he is indeed flesh; yet his days shall be one hundred and twenty years.

Proverbs 18:21

Death and life are in the power of the tongue, And those who love it will eat its fruit.

Job 22:28

You will also declare a thing, And it will be established for you; So light will shine on your ways. You will also declare a thing, And it will be established for you; So light will shine on your ways.

Job 5:12

He disappointeth the devices of the crafty, so that their hands cannot perform their enterprise.

Philippians 4:7

And the peace of God, which transcends all understanding, will guard your hearts and your minds in Christ Jesus.

I write my story for anyone who has suffered anguish, agony, loss, bereavement and for survivors of any type of abuse. I narrate my experiences for children who may have been abandoned and neglected. For the caregivers entrusted to look after them and for the adults who were once children of the state, some of whom I personally know, who have been so courageous and brave during their recovery journey.

I am mindful of people like Bruce Oldfield and Lemn Sissay have emerged out of the care system that did not cater to their needs but yet have achieved quantum degrees of success. They didn't become a statistic and that is huge. I connect with their courage and greatness too.

It is my prayer that my story will encourage, inspire and give hope to the hopeless and minster to some of the most marginalised and oppressed people and for the captives to be set free.

God is a comforter and I can testify to this. I know that one day, not too far from when this book is published, that I will be meeting some of you to share some of my lived experiences through song and the arts. I'm so excited about this.

My narrative is a glimpse into the reality of His Amazing Grace that is unending towards me. The real work of courage and bravery, for me and I think so many other survivors, has been to truly take on a new paradigm. That perspective for me has been to live

out of my God-ordained identity.

As a scholar, I came to learn about different ways that we are socialised and the significance of the family and early life. Because my conditioning was marred by acute deprivation, everything was set up for me to fail. I distrusted others and was hyper-vigilant most of my childhood because my world was very dangerous. I lived in fight or flight, survival mode. It was my coping mechanism. Thanks be to God that when salvation came, the Holy Spirit started to destroy anything toxic from my past. In all honesty, the work of BECOMING is a lifelong journey.

I am a work in progress but as the song says 'this is how I fight my battles'. Interestingly, in me writing my narrative, it's clear that God wanted me to rejoice, sing, shout accolades to him. So you are essentially reading a songbook that I had not planned for. God's ways are clearly not my ways and I've been happy to let Him lead as I write, rejoice and sing. Below is one of my favourite passages that has really inspired me.

Zephania 3:17 This is my favourite passage because knowing that God is a singer is so beautiful to me.

Singing & Rejoicing

God has influenced the writing of my narrative in an extraordinary way, by flooding me with an abundance of songs and of course His intoxicating love.

My story has become a book of rejoicing with some of my most favourite praise and worship pieces. I didn't have a preconceived idea about this, but clearly God had for the overall tone of my book and that was to lift up the name of Jesus.

Part of the vision for my book is to be used in the arts to minister His grace, it is so amazing to see all things working together through my story in such an exuberant way.

John 4:24

There's so much power in rejoicing. Neuroscientists talk about neuroplasticity and neuro-linguistic programming which in summary means the brain is not rigid or concrete. It can be moulded and shaped by the power of thoughts and words. Singing for me is more than what it appears to be at face value. It has been a way for me to rewire my thoughts, connect with the true and living God and express true love and adoration to my9 heavenly Father.

It is a powerful weapon that I have used to change the atmosphere, bring heaven to earth and ultimately shine His light in the darkness causing the enemy to scatter.

I can say that without a shadow of a doubt that worshipping and singing praises to God has been pivotal in the preservation of my life. It has been so very powerful for me in my identity as a Christian because I am becoming who I worship. Those who look to Him are radiant, their faces will never be covered with shame.

Here are some scriptures about singing that really do bless my heart:

Singing of freedom

Psalms 68:6 God sets the lonely in families, he leads out the prisoners with singing; but the rebellious live in a sun-scorched land" Sing of God's love.

Singing of His love

Psalms 89:1 "I will sing of the Lord's great love forever; with my mouth I will make your faithfulness known through all generations".

Singing of what God has done

Sing to him, sing praise to him; tell of all his wonderful acts"

Psalm 105:2 God has done and will continue to do great things in the lives of those who love Him. Our immediate response to Him is lifting up grateful hands and singing a song of praise. Singing allows us the opportunity to speak out about what He has done: broken chains of darkness, forgiven sin, and restored strength to those who are weak.

Sing for joy

Psalm 139:9 "May your priests be clothed with your righteousness; may your faithful people sing for joy".

Sing for your whole life

Psalm 104:33 "I will sing to the Lord all my life; I will sing praise to my God as long as I live".

Sing a new song

Sing to the Lord a new song, his praise from the ends of the earth, you who go down to the sea, and all that is in it, you islands, and all who live in them". Isaiah 42:10

There are new songs to sing to the Lord every day because He is always doing new things in our lives to show His power and presence. We can look to Him to refresh our spirits when we are low with a new song of joy and peace. Our part of this newness is to be aware, humble, and open to what the Lord is doing in our lives.

Sing in times of trouble

About midnight Paul and Silas were praying and singing hymns to God, and the other prisoners were listening to them" (Acts 16:25). Singing in the darkest moments of our lives seems strange. However, it's what God's people should do when we are struggling in literal or emotional prisons. We sing our way free from the bondage of fear and anxiety—in doing so, our faith is strengthened to press forward another day.

Sing with gratitude

"Let the message of Christ dwell among you richly as you teach and admonish one another with all wisdom through psalms, hymns, and songs from the Spirit, singing to God with gratitude in your hearts" (Colossians 3:16)

We have a reason to sing with gratitude to the Lord every time we wake up to a new day filled with grace and mercy. Many times we forget to express our gratefulness in the busyness of our lives. However, we can sing songs of thankfulness for God's goodness to us individually and corporately as a church.

Sing with understanding

"So what shall I do? I will pray with my spirit, but I will also pray with my understanding; I will sing with my spirit, but I will also sing with my understanding" (1 Corinthians 14:15).

When we sing to the Lord, it's more than a beat or rhythm that makes it real. The words we sing must resonate with our understanding of who God is and what He means in our lives. Singing with understanding gives us the connection in our minds and hearts with the beauty of knowing God.

Sing from the heart

"Speaking to one another with psalms, hymns, and songs from the Spirit. Sing and make music from your heart to the Lord" (Ephesians 5:19).

There are many people associated with the knowledge of God in their minds, but they don't know Him in their hearts. So it is with singing to the Lord. In order for us to really connect and know the Lord in song, we must know Him in our hearts. That is, knowing Jesus Christ as Lord and living out His commands.

Sing your Song to God!

Singing rises out of the essence of our souls. We don't have to be trained singers or gifted in singing to raise our voices and hearts to Him in praise. Our thankfulness in the song will lift His name in the presence of saints and sinners. We never know how God will use our singing of personal testimonies to bring someone to Jesus.

The power of singing as a weapon is to demolish negative strongholds can never be understated.

Singing is a great way to magnify God, looking away at what was meant to destroy me and beholding the one who adores me. As I have lifted up praise and worship to magnify the Lord. What you focus on expands, by me focusing on Jesus He has become the centre stage of my life. This has preserved me. I have purposefully cited every word from every song throughout my narrative because it was a way for me to illustrate the power of words in transforming my life, to bring hope, healing, deliverance, breakthrough, inspiration, empowerment and so much more.

This song in particular has blessed me in so many ways.

God I Look to You / Bethel Music

God, I look to You, I won't be overwhelmed

Give me vision to see things like You do

God I look to You, You're where my help comes from

Give me wisdom, You know just what to do

And I will love You, Lord, my strength (sing that out)

I will love You, Lord, my shield

I will love You, Lord, my rock forever

All my days I will love You, God

Yes, I will love You, Lord, my shield

And, I will love You, Lord, my rock forever

All my days I will love You, God

Hallelujah, our God reigns

Hallelujah, our God reigns

Hallelujah, our God reigns

Forever, all my days, Hallelujah

Hallelujah, our God reigns (over every circumstance)

Hallelujah, our God reigns

Oh, Hallelujah, our God reigns

Forever, all my days, Hallelujah

Hallelujah

Songwriters: Ian Bruce Mcintosh / Jenn Louise Johnson

Some more scripture on the power of singing:

God is a singer

Zephania 3:17

The Lord thy God in the midst of thee is mighty; he will save, he will rejoice over thee with joy; he will rest in his love, he will joy over thee with singing.

Colossians 3:16

Let the word of Christ dwell in you richly in all wisdom; teaching and admonishing one another in psalms and hymns and spiritual songs, singing with grace in your hearts to the Lord

1 Chronicles 15:22

And Chenaniah, chief of the Levites, was for song: he instructed about the song, because he was skilful.

God inspired me to highlight this particular song because there is something about affirming what rejoicing does

Surrounded (Fight My Battles) by Michael W. Smith

That's how we fight our battles

This is how I fight my battles

This is how I fight my battles

It may look like I'm surrounded

But I'm surrounded by You

It may look like I'm surrounded

But I'm surrounded by You

What I find incredibly fascinating is that for every obstacle that has been put in my path in the quest for survival, The Lord has blessed me with a breakthrough song. This epiphany comes as I narrate my life story.

It has been quite a process to fathom the abundant, overflowing and eternal love God has graced me with, not having no point of reference in the natural realm.

Today though, I abide in the warmth of who He is to me.

Having not experienced the love of a present earthly father, this letter floods my heart, over and above what a natural dad could ever have done. My initial and my greatest challenge was, could I ever really stand to receive all His love when my earlier life was devoid of family deprivation.

The Father's Love Letter

My Child,

You may not know me, but I know everything about you.

Psalm 139:1

I know when you sit down and when you rise up.

Psalm 139:2

I am familiar with all your ways.

Psalm 139:3

Even the very hairs on your head are numbered.

Matthew 10:29-31

For you were made in my image.

Genesis 1:27

In me you live and move and have your being.

Acts 17:28

For you are my offspring.

Acts 17:28

I knew you even before you were conceived.

Jeremiah 1:4-5

I chose you when I planned creation.

Ephesians 1:11-12

You were not a mistake, for all your days are written in my book.

Psalm 139:15-16

I determined the exact time of your birth and where you would live.

Acts 17:26

You are fearfully and wonderfully made.

Psalm 139:14

I knit you together in your mother's womb.

Psalm 139:13

And brought you forth on the day you were born.

Psalm 71:6

I have been misrepresented by those who don't know me.

John 8:41-44

I am not distant and angry, but am the complete expression of love.

1 John 4:16

And it is my desire to lavish my love on you.

1 John 3:1

Simply because you are my child and I am your Father.

1 John 3:1

I offer you more than your earthly father ever could.

Matthew 7:11

For I am the perfect father.

Matthew 5:48

Every good gift that you receive comes from my hand.

James 1:17

For I am your provider and I meet all your needs.

Matthew 6:31-33

My plan for your future has always been filled with hope.

Jeremiah 29:11

Because I love you with an everlasting love.

Jeremiah 31:3

My thoughts toward you are countless as the sand on the seashore.

Psalm 139:17-18

And I rejoice over you with singing.

Zephaniah 3:17

I will never stop doing good to you.

Jeremiah 32:40

For you are my treasured possession.

Exodus 19:5

I desire to establish you with all my heart and all my soul.

Jeremiah 32:41

And I want to show you great and marvelous things.

Jeremiah 33:3

If you seek me with all your heart, you will find me.

Deuteronomy 4:29

Delight in me and I will give you the desires of your heart.

Psalm 37:4

For it is I who gave you those desires.

Philippians 2:13

I am able to do more for you than you could possibly imagine.

Ephesians 3:20

For I am your greatest encourager.

2 Thessalonians 2:16-17

I am also the Father who comforts you in all your troubles.

2 Corinthians 1:3-4

When you are brokenhearted, I am close to you.

Psalm 34:18

As a shepherd carries a lamb, I have carried you close to my heart.

Isaiah 40:11

One day I will wipe away every tear from your eyes.

Revelation 21:3-4

And I'll take away all the pain you have suffered on this earth.

Revelation 21:3-4

I am your Father, and I love you even as I love my son, Jesus.

John 17:23

For in Jesus, my love for you is revealed.

John 17:26

He is the exact representation of my being.

Hebrews 1:3

He came to demonstrate that I am for you, not against you.

Romans 8:31

And to tell you that I am not counting your sins.

2 Corinthians 5:18-19

Jesus died so that you and I could be reconciled.

2 Corinthians 5:18-19

His death was the ultimate expression of my love for you.

1 John 4:10

I gave up everything I loved that I might gain your love.

Romans 8:31-32

If you receive the gift of my son Jesus, you receive me.

1 John 2:23

And nothing will ever separate you from my love again.

Romans 8:38-39

Come home and I'll throw the biggest party heaven has ever seen.

Luke 15:7

I have always been Father, and will always be Father.

Ephesians 3:14-15

My question is...Will you be my child?

John 1:12-13

I am waiting for you.

Luke 15:11-32

Love, Your Dad.

Almighty God

Delayed but Not Denied

Jeremiah 1:5, "Before I formed you in the womb, I knew you before you were born, I set you apart; I appointed you as a prophet to the nations."

The following song is so poignant for me and for so many reasons. What has brought me to this place of singing love songs to God in worship and adoration is beyond therapeutic. It's divinely healing, for mind, body and spirit. The reason why I have not become a statistic, I credit my love of praising and worshipping God Almighty. Who would have ever thought that indescribable pain and deprivation would cause me to be a worshipper? But God!

More Than Anything / Anita Wilson

Oh

I love You Jesus, I worship and adore You

Just want to tell You, Lord I love You more than anything

Yeah, I love You Jesus, I worship and adore You

Just want to tell You, Lord I love You more than anything

I lift my hands in total adoration unto You

You reign on the throne, for You are God and God alone

Because of You my cloudy days are gone (thank You)

I can sing to You this song

I just want to say that I love You more than anything (come on)

I love You Jesus (I love You Jesus)

Songwriters: Gerald Robinson

My entrance into the world in 1969 was triumphed by a fight of a billion sperm cells. I was the one that made it. I was born a winner.

As a young child, I was taken away from my large family without their consent. It was nothing short of one of the most traumatic experiences I have ever endured that I wouldn't wish on my worst enemy. My childhood was gripped by loss & mourning. It was only when salvation came and I had a dramatic encounter with The Lord, that I became glory struck with the intense fire and power of The Lord's presence. That was in 1997 at a charismatic pentecostal church.

The enemy saw me in the spirit and knew that my original name from birth, Patricia Althia Malcolm carried a particular blessing. Patricia means Noble which is defined in the English Dictionary as "distinguished by rank or title, pertaining to persons so distinguished". Of, belonging to, or constituting a hereditary class that has special social or political status in a country or state; of or pertaining to the aristocracy. Other words to describe my biological name in the dictionary are highborn, aristocratic; patrician, blue-blooded. Of an exalted moral or mental character or excellence: a noble thought and lofty, elevated, high-minded, principled; magnanimous; honourable, estimable, worthy, meritorious. Also, admirable in the dignity of conception, manner of expression, execution, or composition, grand & dignified. These are words to describe just my first name.

Althia means, as explained in the English dictionary, (literally: healing plant), from Greek althein to heal). So my middle name means Healing and is likened to The Rose of Sharon, quite incredible I think, and Malcolm means Peace. So my earthly name can be translated as Honourable Healer of Peace.

This revelation didn't come until three decades later. I began to understand why there was such an attack on my life in the spirit and in the natural to take me out, I mean literally. Decades later it was evident to me, and clear as daylight, why my caregivers refused to call me by the name given to me by my biological mother.

Instead, I was called an unpleasant nick name, the short version of Patricia which meant, i came to find out later, that you get blamed for everything. I answered to this throughout my childhood and even into my adult life. My earlier life experiences literally lived up to this name, and of course, I was none the wiser as to what it meant. All I came to experience and believe was that I was treated as a second class object, inferior, insignificant, and unimportant. I was the one who was labelled and treated in the most derogatory way. Always in the wrong and as you will come to read throughout my story the outcast who was rejected in every way, shape, and form.

God though, had a totally different view of me that would take me 27 years to realise. Today I walk in true royalty as did Esther who was an orphan in the bible.

Esther 4:14 "For if thou altogether holdest thy peace at this time, then shall there enlargement and deliverance arise to the Jews from another place; but thou and thy father's house shall be destroyed: and who knoweth whether thou art come to the kingdom for such a time as this?"

I had a horrible upbringing, but God turned it around for my good. As you read my narrative and I take you on this journey of abandonment, rejection, persecution, shame, identity confusion, racial, emotional, psychological abuse, neglect and what looked like total devastation, I hope you will see the hand of God Almighty at work in my life.

That you, like myself, may have experienced some of the issues my story raises that you will have the courage to receive all the love that you can stand through the power of the Holy Spirit. This takes a lot of bravery and resilience. Sometimes I have not been able to stand with so much loss. God though gave me His strength when I have been weak.

It's the living word that has literally sustained my life. Some of these scriptures I have stood on and they have given me life I think are quite remarkable. They kept me out of the furnace of affliction by giving me real tangible hope.

The Lord has comforted me with some special promises like the ones below that He decreed in His

Word and I can testify that it is because of His word that I am still alive today.

The following scripture is just an example of who I am in Christ:

1 Peter 2:9

But you are a chosen generation, a royal priesthood, a holy nation, His own special people, that you may proclaim the praises of Him who called you out of darkness into His marvellous light;

By the word of God, I was called out of the stigma, shame, a bad name and so forth. I remain in a posture that aligns with my heavenly Father who causes me to walk in dignity, grace and honour.

Duet 8:1 He Said, "Live."

This song "Optimistic" was a song that in my early adult life that was one of my all-time favourites. It literally gripped me to the point that I embodied the energy of the optimism of God. It helped me to stand up and receive all the love that I could stand.

Keep, keep on
Never say die
When in the midst of sorrow
You can' t see up when looking down
A brighter day tomorrow will bring
You hear the voice of reason
Telling you this can't never be done
No matter how hard reality seems
Just hold on to your dreams
Don't give up and don't give in
Although it seems you never win

You will always pass the test

As long as you keep your head to the sky

You can win as long as you keep your head to the sky

You can win as long as you keep your head to the sky

Be Optimistic by The Sounds of Blackness

It wouldn't be until decades later that I'd fully come to understand the real, ugly sometimes demoralizing fight for my life. You see, I came to realize later that according to His word "I was formed before the foundations of the world."

"Before I formed you in the womb, I knew you, and before you were born, I consecrated you; I appointed you a prophet to the nations." Jeremiah 1:5

The enemy knew of this word over my life before I was born and so the fight was on for real, but being the fool that he is, what he failed to take into consideration is that I already have the victory.

If the enemy he had any sense, he would have left me alone. Life to me has been a series of lessons, some enjoyable, some pleasant, some horrible and some agonizing. But I never gave up despite wanting to sometimes. That to me is a testament of Jesus Christ being my keeper. Literally!

What the enemy doesn't realize is that when you touch a child of God, you come against The Almighty. The trials and afflictions have taught me to fight and with that, I have become determined to succeed against all the odds. I cultivated determination, or should I say He grew that in me, along with perseverance, courage and bravery. He has empowered me in such a way that If there weren't trials, I wouldn't have got these

God-given qualities. Here is where one of my favourite scriptures comes to mind.

And from the days of John the Baptist until now the kingdom of heaven suffereth violence, and the violent take it by force. (Mathew 11:12 King James Version)

So there was a command in the spiritual realm, before I was even born, in the atmosphere for me to live as you will see in the scripture below, there was going to be an ugly fight for my life in the spiritual dimension and in the natural.

God knew this before I got here and told me in Mathew 11:12 that there was an attack on the size that I was preordained in, in heaven, which He called the kingdom. He empowered me in His word to take the challenge, the attack, by force.

By listening to His word and destroying the enemy's lies, which has been a challenge at the best of times, I continue to press on and abiding in His word and promises over my life.

I'm trying to give you an idea of the natural and spiritual dimension of the serious warfare I've come into just by being born in this world, and as I was coming through the birth canal, there was a spirit of rejection and abandonment waiting for me on the other side.

Even though I have spent most of my life fighting these spirits in a natural and spiritual dimension, hearing it preached was a whole new ball game. The rejection and abandonment have been so bad at times that I've wanted to leave this world, escape the torture and run away from the pain and have wanted to just go to sleep.

This hasn't been an option though because when the LORD put His hand on me, somehow, as confusing and as dark and bleak as things have been, He causes all things to work together for His Good for those who love Him. His protection over my life is sovereign as the scripture says:

Psalms 91

1 He that dwelleth in the secret place of the most High shall abide under the shadow of the Almighty.

2 I will say of the Lord, He is my refuge and my fortress: my God; in him will I trust.

3 Surely he shall deliver thee from the snare of the fowler, and from the noisome pestilence.

4 He shall cover thee with his feathers, and under his wings shalt thou trust: his truth shall be thy shield and buckler.

5 Thou shalt not be afraid for the terror by night; nor for the arrow that flieth by day;

6 Nor for the pestilence that walketh in darkness; nor for the destruction that wasteth at noonday.

7 A thousand shall fall at thy side, and ten thousand at thy right hand; but it shall not come nigh thee.

8 Only with thine eyes shalt thou behold and see the reward of the wicked.

9 Because thou hast made the Lord, which is my refuge, even the most High, thy habitation;

10 There shall no evil befall thee, neither shall any plague come nigh thy dwelling.

11 For he shall give his angels charge over thee, to keep thee in all thy ways.

12 They shall bear thee up in their hands, lest thou dash thy foot against a stone.

13 Thou shalt tread upon the lion and adder: the young lion and the dragon shalt thou trample under feet.

14 Because he hath set his love upon me, therefore will I deliver him: I will set him on high, because he hath known my name.

15 He shall call upon me, and I will answer him: I will be with him in trouble; I will deliver him, and honour him.

16 With long life will I satisfy him, and shew him my salvation.

This scripture is powerful too

Isaiah 54: 17

"No weapon formed against you shall prosper, And every tongue which rises against you in judgment You shall condemn. This is the heritage of the servants of the Lord, And their righteousness is from Me," Says the Lord.

I am also a living witness of this word over my life too, "And we know that God causes all things to work together for good to those who love God, to those who are called according to His purpose". (Romans 8:28. King James Version)

It's because of songs like the one below and the love and grace so richly infused in this gospel anthem that helped me stand up despite feeling so weak. Despite my internal weather being dense and gloomy, this song with all its warmth, passion, anointing, blessedness and power, helped me not only stand but to go so far as to dance in the holy spirit in service in the presence of Lord. Hallelujah!

The resonance of this song emanated on a bright hot summer day aglow with the power of God. I look forward to meeting some of my readers in person and rejoice and sing together to celebrate my life through the arts. This following celebratory anthem always warms my heart. Especially as it's sung in patois.

I've got my mind made up and I won't turn back

Because I want to see my Jesus someday

I've got my mind made up and I won't turn back

Because I want to see my Jesus someday

I've got my mind made up and I won't turn back

Because I want to see my Jesus someday

I've got my mind made up and I won't turn back

Because I want to see my Jesus someday

Goodbye world, I stay no longer with you

Goodbye pleasures of sin, I stay no longer with you

I've made up my mind to go God's way the rest of my life

I've made up my mind to go God's way the rest of my life

Goodbye world, I stay no longer with you

Goodbye pleasures of sin, I stay no longer with you

I've made up my mind to go God's way the rest of my life

I've made up my mind to go God's way the rest of my life

Born, born, born again thank God, I'm born again

Born, born, born again thank God, I'm born again

Born, born, born again thank God, I'm born again

Born, born, born again thank God, I'm born again

Born of the water, spirit and the blood thank God, I'm born again

Born of the water, spirit and the blood thank God, I'm born again

Born of the water, spirit and the blood thank God, I'm born again

Born of the water, spirit and the blood thank God, I'm born again

I've got my mind made up and I won't turn back

Because I want to see my Jesus someday

I've got my mind made up and I won't turn back

Because I want to see my Jesus someday

I am under the rock, the rock that's higher than I

Jehovah hide me, I am under the rock

Go tell my enemies, I am under the rock

Jehovah hide me, I am under the rock

Jesus name so sweet, Emanuel name so sweet

Jesus name so sweet, Emanuel name so sweet

Jesus name so sweet, Emanuel name so sweet

Jesus name so sweet, Emanuel name so sweet

Every rock, me rock upon Jesus Jesus' name so sweet

Every rock, me rock upon Jesus Jesus' name so sweet

Every rock, me rock upon Jesus Jesus' name so sweet

Every rock, me rock upon Jesus Jesus' name so sweet

I've got my mind made up and I won't turn back

Because I want to see my Jesus someday

I've got my mind made up and I won't turn back

Because I want to see my Jesus someday

Oh, I want to see Him, look upon His face

There, to sing forever of His saving grace

On the streets of glory let me lift my voice

All my cares are past, home at last, ever to rejoice

Yes, I want to see Him, wanna look upon His face

There, to sing forever of His saving grace

On the streets of glory let me lift my voice

All my cares are past, home at last, ever to rejoice

I've got my mind made up and I won't turn back

Because I want to see my Jesus someday

I've got my mind made up and I won't turn back

Because I want to see my Jesus someday

I've got my mind made up and I won't turn back

Because I want to see my Jesus someday

I've got my mind made up and I won't turn back

Because I want to see my Jesus someday

Fire, fire, fire, fire fall on me

Fire, fire, fire, fire fall on me

On the day of Pentecost, the fire fall on me

On the day of Pentecost, the fire fall on me

Fire, fire, fire, fire fall on me

By Donnie McClurkin

The following passage reads as a hopeless case scenario, but for the grace of God at least towards the end of the passage there was a command made by God to live.

Ezekiel 16:4 "And as for your birth, on the day you were born your navel cord was not cut, nor were you washed with water to cleanse you, nor rubbed with salt or swaddled with bands at all". 5 No eye pitied you to do any of these things for you, to have compassion on you; but you were cast out in the open field, for your person was abhorrent and loathsome on the day that you were born. 6 And when I passed by you and saw you rolling about in your blood, I said to you in your blood, Live! Yes, I said to you still in your natal blood, Live! 7 I caused you [Israel] to multiply as the bud which grows in the field, and you increased and became tall, and you came to full maidenhood and beauty; your breasts were formed, and your hair had grown, yet you were naked and bare. 8 Now I passed by you again and looked upon you; behold, you were maturing and at the time for love, and I spread My skirt over you and covered your nakedness. Yes, I plighted My troth to you and entered into a covenant with you, says the Lord, and you became Mine. 9 Then I washed you with water; yes, I thoroughly washed away your [clinging] blood from you and I anointed you with oil. 10 I clothed you also with embroidered cloth and shod you with [fine seal] leather, and I girded you about with fine linen and covered you with silk. 11 I decked you also with ornaments, and I put bracelets on your wrists and a chain on your neck.

"Where's My Mama Gone"?

Deuteronomy 31:6 Be strong and of a good courage, fear not, nor be afraid of them: for the Lord thy God, he it is that doth go with thee; he will not fail thee, nor forsake thee.

There just were no words as an infant being torn away from my family! Just no words. Later in life, I was comforted by this powerful passage in Psalms 27 which says,

1 "The Lord is my light and my salvation; whom shall I fear? the Lord is the strength of my life; of whom shall I be afraid"? 2 When the wicked, even mine enemies and my foes, came upon me to eat up my flesh, they stumbled and fell. 3 Though an host should encamp against me, my heart shall not fear: though war should rise against me, in this will I be confident. 4 One thing

have I desired of the Lord, that will I seek after; that I may dwell in the house of the Lord all the days of my life, to behold the beauty of the Lord, and to enquire in his temple. 5 For in the time of trouble he shall hide me in his pavilion: in the secret of his tabernacle shall he hide me; he shall set me up upon a rock. 6 And now shall mine head be lifted up above mine enemies round about me: therefore will I offer in his tabernacle sacrifices of joy; I will sing, yea, I will sing praises unto the Lord. 7 Hear, O Lord, when I cry with my voice: have mercy also upon me, and answer me. 8 When thou saidst, Seek ye my face; my heart said unto thee, Thy face, Lord, will I seek. 9 Hide not thy face far from me; put not thy servant away in anger: thou hast been my help; leave me not, neither forsake me, O God of my salvation. 10 When my father and my mother forsake me, then the Lord will take me up. 11 Teach me thy way, O Lord, and lead me in a plain path, because of mine enemies. 12 Deliver me not over unto the will of mine enemies: for false witnesses are risen up against me, and such as breathe out cruelty. 13 I had fainted, unless I had believed to see the goodness of the Lord in the land of the living. 14 Wait on the Lord: be of good courage, and he shall strengthen thine heart: wait, I say, on the Lord.

It was as if I was a bird singing on the fragile branch of an alien tree in a strange land far away. The smell in the house was sterile, empty, hollow, and void of soul. It was different from Nan's house. Very! It wasn't home. Where was I?

I sang "where's my mama gone, where's my mama gone, where's my mama gone, where's my mama gone, far away" and did so at the top of my lungs. I wanted to go home.

At such a tender age of four, I sang out to a higher order, a realm that can be tapped into that brings comfort to a torn soul in a wretched world. That somehow by looking up into the sky and belting out a song about my absent mama I was expecting heaven to provide the huge piece of the missing puzzle that was gone. I wondered if God smiled and searched the clouds for the missing part.

God seemed to frown as grey clouds gathered together in a concerted mood that was sorrowful and bleak. The more overcast it got, the more I sang aloud as if my tiny voice from my small four-year-old frame could somehow change the dull grey atmosphere and gloom to a ray of warm, bright and healing sunshine.

It never did, and instead of things getting better, I was about to begin a long journey of such pain and suffering, that only God himself can get the credit for preserving and keeping me intact. This is my story, and I openly, unashamedly and wholeheartedly lift up my eyes to where my help came from because it comes from the Lord.

Psalm 121

1 I will lift up my eyes unto the hills, from whence cometh my help. 2 My help cometh from the Lord, which made heaven and earth. 3 He will not suffer thy foot to be moved: he that keepeth thee will not slumber. 4 Behold, he that keepeth Israel shall neither slumber nor sleep. 5 the lord is thy keeper: the LORD is thy shade upon thy right hand. 6 The sun shall not smite thee by day, nor the moon by night. 7 The LORD shall preserve thee from all evil: he shall preserve thy soul. 8 The LORD shall keep thy going out and thy coming in from this time forth, and even forevermore. King James Version

The reality was that I was in captivity and far away from a place called home and perched on a window ledge behind a net curtain. It was my safety net, a place where I could hide away from this alien world. Everything was strange, the people weren't the same colour as me, they sounded different, ate strange food and their ways seemed peculiar.

I searched the atmosphere around me for some source of comfort, anything. A homely smell of Caribbean food cooking in the kitchen, but there was none, my eyes sought to locate some vibrant, warm colours, but they weren't there either. I yearned and longed to be comforted with a sense of home but found nothing.

Singing where I was, connected me to the music in my spirit. The sounds and rhythms I created were as If I were entertaining angels that I invited to come and play with me in another dimension, oblivious to the naked eye. The melodic sounds I sang travelled through the net curtain and boomeranged back. It was as if love travelled out of my heart and through my spirit leaving my body, to then circle back to me in the form of a spiritual hug. This wrapped around my tiny frame in the form of a colourful rainbow.

I was happy to sing that song about the whereabouts of my mama because the people around me were my captors, singing gave me relief. It was 1973 and I was living in a children's home. Dixton was the name of the place, a huge house with no soul, it felt like a hollow cavity. I was with lots of other neglected children around my age. The rooms were gigantic, I was like this tiny kid dwarfed in what seemed like a hollow shell.

Even though the house was full of kids and care workers there was nothing in the environment that warmed my heart other than my love of singing. The atmosphere was clinical, and everything within it was alien. My family had become a distant memory so much so that I lost all concept of family life.

And The Truth Shall Set You Free

The below song has really ministered to me

Who You Say I Am / Hillsong Worship

Who am I that the highest King Would welcome me?

I was lost but He brought me in Oh His love for me Oh His love for me

Who the Son sets free Oh is free indeed I'm a child of God Yes I am

Free at last, He has ransomed me His grace runs deep While I was a slave to sin

Jesus died for me Yes He died for me Who the Son sets free Oh is free indeed

I'm a child of God Yes I am In my Father's house

There's a place for me I'm a child of God Yes I am I am chosen Not forsaken

I am who You say I am You are for me Not against me I am who You say I am

I am chosen Not forsaken I am who You say I am You are for me Not against me

I am who You say I am I am who You say I am

Who the Son sets free Oh is free indeed I'm a child of God

Yes I am In my Father's house There's a place for me I'm a child of God

Yes I am In my Father's house There's a place for me I'm a child of God Yes I am

My aunt gave her version of what happened to me by saying "da people dem come to an tek uno an teef you" she said in her Jamaican patois, cockney accent. Your aunties were looking after uno, then her emphasis shifting into cockney slang, that woman, Jackie, she shouted the name as the social worker's name fell out of her mouth with an aggressive bang, and took yah.

Anger filled my aunt's front room like an uninvited guest to a family get together.

When mama (my nan) came home from work and saw you weren't there she went straight to the social services office to take you back home. Her tone was aggressive, angry and hurt, and as she took another swig of beer as if to comfort herself. She poured me a drink of beer, it was bitter and tasted strange. But I got used to drinking with my aunt as I came to associate beer, alcohol, cigarettes and reggae music with a reward of family time, attention, affection, and love.

"They refused to give you back and put you in the home in the country, and we never saw you again".

By age eleven I was on my third move. In just eleven years I had gone from my family home to a children's home in Barnet. Hertfordshire to a foster placement in Hoddesdon. Hertfordshire to a children's home in

Finsbury Park, Islington. All in the space of eleven years.

By this time I thought I was finished, but God had other ideas. Despite my young age I looked out at the world with peculiar wisdom inhabited by an old, worn, tried, abused and battered soul. I didn't trust the world or the inhabitants in it. It was a dangerous, hostile, lonely, and confusing place to be. Somehow, on that day when I was sitting in my aunt's house, some love managed to ease its way into my guarded soul. The sunlight forced its way through the cracks of a prison of my being that was heavily guarded.

My aunt told me of the trips that she used to make to the home with Nan and my other aunt. They came to plait my hair and bring me new clothes. But my aunt said in her patios English, "when we used to com bac an see you, you never had on the pretty dresses that mama (nan) used to bring for you.

Mama said, (my aunt imitating nan's voice), " where de clothes mi come bring uno, where dem de? My aunt said, I always looked nervous, like I wanted to speak but wasn't comfortable to do so. She and mama (nan) sensed something was wrong, but they couldn't put their finger on it. Something wasn't right, the people at home looking after me definitely couldn't be trusted. My aunt said I used to look scared. It would be a few decades before nan gave me her version of what happened.

Another aunt was at home with me in the house, looking after me when the social worker came and knocked on the door and asked where my nan was. They told her that she was at work and the next thing they knew I was being taken away by the social services. When my nan came home to find me, and I was not there, she ran to the office to get me back, but they said that because my nan was working all day that I would not be able to go back with her. Nan said she would stop working, but they refused.

This is where forgiveness comes in and yes, it is an ongoing theme. When He commands you to forgive there's no compromise. When it's hard to do as it has been for me, I just cry out to him and say HELP ME JESUS!!!

Many years later, I was able to read some of my records to see the truth. I was taken away because there were no adults looking after me. Quite a sobering fact to find out.

When salvation came in 1997 I experienced the real truth of God's love through His word. Darkness, in my case the abandonment and neglect, could not comprehend the light. He began to overcompensate all the deprivation I had experienced in my former years.

John 1:5 And the light shines in the darkness, and the darkness did not comprehend it. His dazzling light, His power, presence, glory and splendour overwhelmed the shame, despair, sadness that I was formerly all too familiar with.

CSI Barnet

Deuteronomy 31:6 "Be strong and courageous. Do not be afraid or terrified because of them, for the Lord your God goes with you; he will never leave you nor forsake you."

Nan said that she and granddad came out to Barnet to take me home, both of them were determined that they were not going to live without me. They came to take me back home, but the people working at the children's home called the police out, and granddad was arrested. Can you believe it, they arrested Him.

It wasn't until later on when I was doing life story work with Corby, my lovely social worker (an earth angel) that I came to be aware that, maybe I was a wanted child, maybe my family did love me. But, as a child who had experienced life as a living hell, abused and misused, I never felt accepted, cared for or loved, it was challenging for my mind to take it all in.

Corby later broke protocol to help ignite the poet, writer, and beauty that was placed deep down in my inner being. The bible says to be mindful that you may entertain angels among strangers. Hebrew 13:2

My younger brother, joined me at Dixton when he was eighteen months old, and before you knew it, we were out in the sticks in Hertfordshire with the Hamilton's. Life was about to get a whole lot worse. My brother and I were about to nearly lose our lives.

The house looked like a picture box on the outside. It was set on a road called Rye Park in Hoddesdon, Hertfordshire that overlooked the vast park and playing fields adjacent to my then primary school. It was a standard three-bedroom white house with green shutters that dressed the periphery of the four equally spaced external windows. What I was about to endure in that house robbed me so much of my innocence that I lost my joy and the very essence of who I was.

This was not home nor the people who lived in it a family. My foster father was a dark-haired man of medium build with brown eyes. He was in his early thirties. His wife Doreen was most unusual to what I'd ever known as a child. She was in her early thirties, petite, maybe five foot two . Between them, they had a daughter, a toddler who's name was Maxine. She was the favourite with big brown eyes, long brown hair and the "adorable" one. What a strange composition of a family. Me with my parched mahogany ashy skin that literally looked grey from the neglect of skin cream. My hair was all cut off, Just my image alone you would have thought that someone may have stepped in to intervene, but I was in no man's land. There was my gorgeous brother Richard of eighteen months who was so adorable too.

I was given second-hand clothes from the jumble sale bought with the allowance that Doreen and Mick got for looking after me. I'm sure they used that money to fund their holiday trips abroad to Spain that I never went to. They'd take me to their parent's house, an elderly couple and I'd stay there while the Hamilton's travelled around the Mediterranean.

Maxine got lovely shoes and accessories and clothing, but I got second-hand everything from the jumble sale, including shoes that were two sizes too small. It was these horrible shoes that caused me to walk on the edge of my feet, I was like a crippled child

What my brother and I experienced in that house was so so hard.

Flashing Lights & Shattered Crystal

This Holy Spirit led me to cite this song here and I think the reason why is because regardless of such harrowing life events His blood will never lose its power. It washed me clean, made me a new creature in Christ and what was meant to destroy me the blood of Christ made me strong and fortified me. I came out of this chapter of my life literally by His grace.

There Is Power in the Blood / Alan Jackson

There is power, power, wonder-working power In the blood of the Lamb
There is power, power, wonder-working power In the precious blood of the Lamb

There is power, power, wonder-working power In the blood of the Lamb

There is power, power, wonder-working power In the precious blood of the Lamb

Songwriters: Alan Jackson

By His grace, I have been able to write this chapter of my story with the illumination and wisdom in His word. The following passages have literally been my strength when I was so weak.

Psalms 24:7

Lift up your heads, O you gates! And be lifted up, you everlasting doors! And the King of glory shall come in.

2 Corinthians 4:17

For our light affliction, which is but for a moment, is working for us a far more exceeding and eternal weight of glory,

Psalm 46:1

God is our refuge and strength, a very present help in trouble.

Revelation 12:11

And they overcame him by the blood of the Lamb and by the word of their testimony, and they did not love their lives to the death.

His Good met my bad which the darkness could not comprehend. When salvation came the light outshone what was pre-existing, every glory has a story.

John 1:5 And the light shines in the darkness, and the darkness did not comprehend it.

My brother ended up in the hospital at eighteen months on life support. My world fell apart as If I became a broken, lifeless raggedy doll. There was no essence to life left to live anymore. My brother was hospitalized in intensive care. It would not be until years later when I was in care at the children's homes in Finsbury Park that I'd get to see my brother for a contact visit at Dixton.

The foster people took me up the huge stairs of this massive hospital. I was four years old and to this day remember the distinct hospital smell of the children's ward. It was strange. As I walked towards the enormous cot, nan who I'd not seen for a long time walked towards me, she said in her loving, soft patios voice, " what happened"?.

I was confused, perplexed, and disorientated at the time. Before we could even speak or exchange any hugs, I was ushered away from my aunts and nan to the outside of my brother's cot that resembled a spaghetti junction on a motorway with miles of tubes. That would be the last time I would see nan until I was eleven years old and back in care in Finsbury Park some seven years later. My soul was destroyed.

I couldn't see my brother beyond all the equipment around his cot. I just didn't know what to make of any of it. I'm four years old and staring at this cot with my baby brother. Dazed. Numb.

That was my brother there, I wanted to touch him, smell him, wrap him up like a dolly and take him home, but that was the last time I was with him for a good ten years. I was heartbroken and wept inside like those willow trees that bow down to the ground, the branches and leaves descending terrain as if grief-stricken with pain. I was a walking miracle and not aware of the inner strength I was carrying. It wouldn't be until twenty-three years later when God revealed to me what I was carrying and why I had to go through what I had to go through.

I didn't understand my brother's trauma until I was put into care in London and doing life story work with a social worker who was to become a friend and confidant. She was safe. She showed me genuine acceptance and love, and we had a real bond. The beginning of signs and wonders.

Despite my brother's near fatality, I was left to live with the Hamilton's for some odd reason. Was another accident waiting to happen? What was about to take place left me at the brink of death's door.

Being estranged and torn from my biological family left me in a constant state of loss and mourning. The normality of my life was darkness, trauma, and isolation. Being the only black child in the family I was alienated from the clan and was ill-treated. All my hair was cut off and I was devoid of tender loving care.

I remember one day when we were at dinner and I was being served an unsightly portion of fat from meat to eat with vegetables while Maxine, Doreen, Mick, and Maxine had a hearty colourful plate of food. My eyes welled up, and my stomach began to regurgitate at the smell and sight of gristle, and grime on the plate. I couldn't even cry. " I don't want it......I can't eat it," I painfully voiced. "If you don't eat," Doreen said in her mean spiteful voice a, "you'll have to stand in the corner and say sorry a hundred times."

I thought I'd instead go to bed without dinner than eat a plate of food that you wouldn't even feed to a dog. So I went into the corner and said I'm sorry for what seemed to be forever until my belly was literally grumbling from hunger, but the pain was more natural to bear than looking at what was on that plate.

Living out a cursed name that Hamilton spoke over my life was a living nightmare. Life wasn't worth living. I was a living and walking corpse, alive by default but dead inside. God couldn't let me die because He purposed for me to receive salvation, knowing that I would become obsessed with His amazing love and ultimately an evangelist sharing the passion of The Christ. My mess was to become my message and He was going to turn my scars into stars.

When I received the Lord in 1997, I rebuked the cursed nickname that was given by the abusers and I only answered to Patricia, the precious name on my birth certificate, which as I said earlier means noble, highborn, aristocratic, honourable, grand, exalted, lordly, majestic, queenly. God clearly had a plan for my life, giving me such an anointed name like that. It's only when I look back now that I can partly see why there was such an attack on my life.

The incredible thing here is that I can clearly see, now that I am looking back, is that God was setting me up to win. The fight was a fixed fight and still is. It is just that the real, living hell that crushed, broke and nearly left me dead was a process that I endured to encourage others. That could be you, who's in desperate need of a word of encouragement, for me to tell you that you are going to make it. If I don't look like my circumstances, I can tell you that you are not your circumstances because Christ is "bigger" than your trials and afflictions.

This passage too is one that has breathed life into me. Galatians 2:20 "I have been crucified with Christ; it is no longer I who live, but Christ lives in me; and the life which I now live in the flesh I live by faith in the Son of God, who loved me and gave Himself for me". He promised to do "exceeding abundantly above all that we ask or think, according to the power that worketh in us" Ephesians 3:20.

My musings!

God will never let you suffer and endure without the promise of giving you something higher than what you had before. See later chapter on signs, wonders, and miracles as to how God used my hell to be a footstool, a springboard into my destiny and purpose. It was a womb that birthed the greatness in me. He said what the devil meant for evil I'm gonna turn it around for your good.

But as for you, ye thought evil against me; but God meant it unto good, to bring to pass, as it is this day, to save many people alive. Genesis 5:20 King James Version

If the Son, therefore, makes you free, ye shall be free indeed. John 8:36. King James Bible

SHINY RED SHOES FOR THE YELLOW BRICK

1 Peter 5:10

And after you have suffered a little while, the God of all grace, who has called you to his eternal glory in Christ, will himself restore, confirm, strengthen, and establish you.

Romans 8:18

For I consider that the sufferings of this present time are not worth comparing with the glory that is to be revealed to us.

Romans 5:3-5

More than that, we rejoice in our sufferings, knowing that suffering produces endurance, and endurance produces character, and character produces hope, and hope does not put us to shame, because God's love has been poured into our hearts through the Holy Spirit who has been given to us.

Romans 8:28

And we know that for those who love God all things work together for good, for those who are called according to his purpose.

James 1:2-4

Count it all joy, my brothers, when you meet trials of various kinds, for you know that the testing of your faith produces steadfastness. And let steadfastness have its full effect, that you may be perfect and complete, lacking in nothing.

John 16:33

I have said these things to you, that in me you may have peace. In the world, you will have tribulation. But take heart; I have overcome the world."

I have come to see that the attack that I endured at eleven years of age was the enemy trying to curtail my life journey. But this violation that you are about to read is the very area where God promised to bless me. He calls my precious feet beautiful to preach. I was going to need divine intervention to be able to receive " All The Love I Could Stand" to walk this promise out over my life.

Isaiah 52:7

How beautiful upon the mountains Are the feet of him who brings good news, Who proclaims peace, Who brings glad tidings of good things, Who proclaims salvation, Who says to Zion, "Your God reigns!"

This song has become a powerful anthem for me. It is because of His love that I am able to stand on my feet even if they were brutally attacked as a child. As I have forgiven the oppressors who were cruel to me I am free to stand in the power of His love and worship Him with this song which I often sing in my prayer closet.

Reckless Love

Written by Cory Asbury, Caleb Culver, and Ran Jackson

Verse 1

Before I spoke a word, You were singing over me

You have been so, so good to me

Before I took a breath, You breathed Your life in me

You have been so, so kind to me

Chorus

Oh, the overwhelming, never-ending, reckless love of God

Oh, it chases me down, fights 'til I'm found, leaves the ninety-nine

I couldn't earn it, I don't deserve it, still You give Yourself away

Oh, the overwhelming, never-ending, reckless love of God

Verse 2

When I was Your foe, still Your love fought for me

You have been so, so good to me

When I felt no worth, You paid it all for me

You have been so, so kind to me

Bridge

There's no shadow You won't light up

Mountain You won't climb up

Coming after me

There's no wall You won't kick down

Lie You won't tear down

Coming after me

When Doreen used to buy new clothes for Maxine and buy mine from the jumble sale with the handsome foster care allowance that she got, it confused me. I learned that I was only worthy of second-hand treatment. Was it because I was a different colour? Was I too ugly, didn't I deserve cute clothes and nice shoes? I cried inside!

I felt like the parched brown paper bag that my mum used that time to wrap her can of strong beer in when we had to stop on the motorway that day en route to see my brother in Aylesbury. My dry and unloved skin hurt but I became used to the discomfort and the pain became the norm. I didn't know what cream or moisturizer felt like. Instead of my skin looking like beautiful brown luxurious chocolate, it was ashy, grey, itchy and uncomfortable, and my hair? Well, it was all cut off and what was there was brittle.

When I look at photographs of me at that time, I see an uncared for child with all life ebbing away. It wasn't until Hamilton's put up a French Caribbean lady as a lodger for one weekend that I came to realize at eight years old that my hair deserved some TLC. I don't remember her name, but she had a lovely smile, she was warm, friendly, and majestic-looking and as soon as she set her eyes on me she fell in love with me.

She asked Doreen for some hair oil, Doreen looked at her puzzled, confused, lost, as if the lady was talking another language. "hair oil" she replied! Clearly, she didn't understand. Well, do you know the lady ended up using lard on my hair to bring some sort of relief? Was she sent from God, if He existed? I mean if He were real and loved me, he wouldn't allow me to suffer such intense trauma, but maybe?

One day Doreen came home from the jumble sale with a special present for me, well, so she implied. As I had lost all hope by this point in my childhood, I came to associate "something special" with something not nice and boy was I right, I just didn't know that I was about to start one of the most crippling journeys of my life.

I really didn't like the look of those shiny red shoes with all those straps. They looked crippling with the two-inch heel. Was Doreen really going to make me wear them, I had no fight in me to even say anything. They were two sizes too small, and I was unable to walk in them.

Doreen put it down to the patent leather being nearly new and that with wear the stiff hard material that imprisoned my feet would relax and get softer. She actually began to comment aloud that I wasn't walking correctly. When I took the shoes off, my toes were so sore I had to walk on the sides of my soles.

These horrible shoes spoke of the broken life that I was living. Broken emotionally through the tears of pain, grief, and sadness and loss of my biological family. My innocence was shattered, and it took away my preciousness. My racial identity had been spoiled, and there was no hope in sight of recovering my identity, other than an empty dream of the lady from France coming back as a ray of hope. Is this how Victoria Climbe felt when she was being abused? After all, there were so many people, teachers, neighbours, social workers, family associates, and friends that were part of that child's world. At that time, I, like her, appeared invisible.

Being the only black child in a white neighbourhood I felt unseen, that I was nonexistent, a spare part that served its purpose. I was a commodity that's sole purpose was to provide a generous income for the Hamilton's and to supplement the part-time cleaning jobs that they did in the evening.

They must have made quite a lot of money because every Christmas and summer, Doreen, Mick and their daughter Maxine travelled somewhere to Spain or somewhere nice and hot. I stayed at Doreen's mum and dad's house. I was under the care of an old frail, and elderly couple with a small house in Hemel Hempstead who I suppose did their best.

At least I wasn't locked away in a bedroom as I sometimes was with the Hamilton's when they used to go out and do nice things. At their parent's house, I was free, wasn't given the fat of the food to eat, didn't have to worry that Mick was going catch me in the house. didn't have to wear crippling red shoes and wasn't called derogatory names like 'thicky" or being called a "dustbin" at the dinner table.

Life was so unkind, I felt like a mistake, and all I wanted to do was die. On their return, there was talk in the air about an operation on my feet to correct the deformities of bones that had not had room to grow.

That surgeon's knife would come to be one of the most excruciating experiences of my life ever when I was to return back to care at eleven years of age. In a system that although allowed me to escape from Hamilton's hostility I was about to suffer from a physical pain that was so excruciating that the fact that I survived alone is a testament that there is a God. Not my thoughts at the time, though. I was in a living hell.

It seemed like it was not going to be a smooth transition either as I remember one day when Doreen was at home, and on the lounge on the phone, she had let me go and play out on my bike unsupervised. As I was cycling beyond the garden and in the concrete car park, I don't know how this happened, but as I pulled on the brakes my whole body flung over the handlebars, and my body crashed into the concrete leaving me temporarily without oxygen. My lungs had all the air deflated from them. I thought it was over.

I don't know how I managed to crawl from the car park through the garden, into the house on all fours clinging to dear, precious life but at the same time feeling like I was fighting a losing battle. I just made it through from the kitchen, to the first lounge past the stairway and slumped on the floor to the visibility of Doreen who was on the phone.

Not sparing any time to say goodbye to who she was talking to, she dropped the phone down and ran over to me, screamed oh my God. Do you know, I don't know what happened after that, I must have backed out, the rest is really a blur, all I can say is that my survival of that near fatality was a miracle.

The Brown Paper Bag

One day my my social worker, a thin english man of medium height dressed in a brown worn corduroy jacket and trousers to match with an old worn shirt came to pick me up in Hertfordshire to go and see my estranged brother. I wondered what he looked like now, my last memory of him was in a hospital cot. I got in the back of the car, my mum was in the front of the car, I wondered who that lady was? I'd only met her once before in a supervised visit at a family centre, and that was really hard. I mean, imagine you haven't seen your biological mother in years, I was looking at someone I didn't know!

How do you pour out all your hurt to a stranger, we didn't know how to hug each other much less love, and nobody had taught me love and affection, I mean I was there as a broken child, Life had taught me not to trust or open up, it was full of traps devoid of love just trauma, abuse and pain. All I remember that day as we were driving on the motorway to see my brother, he said to my mum what's in the brown paper bag? All I could see from the back seat was that she had something inside it as she took a drink from something in the bag. Robert asked her to stop drinking but she continued. He pulled the car over, got out, came over to the front passenger seat and opened the car door. By that time the drink had been consumed, we ended up taking a U turn, so that was that.

Can you imagine how I felt on the initial encounter I had with my mum a few years before where we were sitting opposite each other with a strange person supervising our contact in the room, and my mum just sat there and saying negative things to me. I felt ugly and unloved and hurt that this woman who was supposed to be my mother could be so cold and she had been drinking too.

My social worker came to see me one day and took me into the lounge that was rarely used in the Hamilton's house. He asked me if I like living at the foster house? "Well", I said, "I'm not part of the family". He looked down as if sensing my hidden trauma. Two weeks later he came to pick me up and a weathered suitcase. He pulled down the boot door of the car. The sun shone from a blue celestial sky that day and as I waited to get in the car the fresh air caressed my face, and I breathed in hope on what was about to be a new era for me at the central turning point of my life. Doreen said goodbye, as I put the seat belt on and looked out of the window to wave goodbye, she appeared to have a tear in her eye. I didn't understand!

I was numb, saying goodbye. It was strange, but in all honesty, I never felt loved or protected by Doreen, and we didn't exactly have a mother-daughter bond. I just served the purpose of helping her to get an income for her and her family, much like the slaves working on the cotton fields served as a commodity that produced income for their slave masters. So goodbye it was, and I was on my way to Islington where the family that I had been torn away from were living. It had been seven years since I was last in London and a lot had happened that my family were oblivious too and I had no language to say what had happened.

The Messenger

The words to this particular song have brought me so much love and comfort that it gives me security that no other entity could.

God I Look to You / Bethel Music

God, I look to You, I won't be overwhelmed

Give me vision to see things like You do

God I look to You, You're where my help comes from

Give me wisdom, You know just what to do

God, I look to You, I won't be overwhelmed

Give me vision to see things like You do

God I look to You, You're where my help comes from

Give me wisdom, You know just what to do

And I will love You, Lord, my strength (sing that out)

I will love You, Lord, my shield

I will love You, Lord, my rock forever

All my days I will love You, God

Hallelujah, our God reigns

Hallelujah, our God reigns

Hallelujah, our God reigns

Forever, all my days, Hallelujah

Songwriters: Ian Bruce Mcintosh / Jenn Louise Johnson

Truth be told I was so so cast down at this time in my childhood, it looked like a hopeless situation but God ensured I wasn't totally finished off and this scripture speaks to me of His total power,

2 Corinthians 4:9 Cast Down but Unconquered

But we have this treasure in earthen vessels, that the excellence of the power may be of God and not of us. We are hard-pressed on every side, yet not crushed; we are perplexed, but not in despair; persecuted, but not forsaken; struck down, but not destroyed— always carrying about in the body the dying of the Lord Jesus, that the life of Jesus also may be manifested in our body. For we who live are always delivered to death for Jesus' sake, that the life of Jesus also may be manifested in our mortal flesh.

My new home was 3 Elwood Street, off Blackstock road in Highbury near Finsbury Park in the borough of Islington. It was a small four-bedroom house that didn't look like a children's home. The superintendent that worked there was called Murial, an English white lady and another lady who worked there called Wendy.

I was the only black girl there. There were two English boys there, Paul and his brother. Their mother used to come and visit them regularly. I was in unfamiliar territory, the food was horrible. I distinctly remember being served boiled wet cabbage with other tasteless food. I remember every Saturday I used to get pocket money and the highlight of that would be buying sweets and crisps from the shop. That's the only thing that saved me. My overall feeling about Elwood street was Ugh, just UGGHHH!!!!!!!!!!!!

Robert, my then social worker, came to inform me one day that an operation had been organized for me to undergo. Strangely, it was a hospital in Hertfordshire, I was told the reason for this was because Hamilton's had arranged it. My thinking at the time was I didn't have a choice whether to go under the knife, after all, I was eleven, with no voice. The only voice I did have as a child was on the one occasion when Robert asked me when I was living at Hamilton's as if I was happy. I responded to him by saying that I was in the family but not a part of it and that was the only time my voice was ever heard as a child.

My voice was taken away from me about having an operation. NO WORDS!!!!

Prior to the operation, like a few weeks before there were new kids that had come to stay in the home. One of them was a girl called Donna, a fair chubby girl with a golden afro and brown-green eyes. We soon became friends, she was like my buddy.

Within no time at all, I remember lying in a hospital bed with the bed slanted, so that my head was tipped backwards. I came around looking at the white ceiling, my eyes were welled up with tears. I was so scared. I heard elderly people talking. There was a lady (a messenger, I believe) to my right who must have listened to my sobs, she must have been visiting her relative. She turned to me with a handful of tissues and wiped my tear-stained face dry. Although she didn't speak her disposition, gestures and actions reassured me that although no one was with me, I wasn't completely disregarded and abandoned.

In record time, I was back at Elwood street and on crutches, but I was about to live an unparalleled nightmare. It was a cold rainy day, and Wendy was on duty. She asked us, kids, if we wanted to go up to Finsbury Park to the shops. I said that I didn't want to go because my feet were bandaged in huge swabs of dressing, but my voice didn't count.

She got some plastic bags and tied them around my hugely bandaged feet that resembled two footballs. I must have been a right sight and a laughing stock. I was made to walk in the rain to and from Finsbury Park with that woman and the other kids. The trauma, humiliation, and pain was real but surreal. On the way home every step I took was a sloppy sludge of wet cotton wool and bandages.

I went to the bathroom, deflated, ejected, broken and traumatized. Life wasn't worth living anymore! I unwrapped my bandages for the first time and saw my raw wounds from the surgery with three metal pins around each big toe. I sat on the edge of the bath looking down at the wrangled mess of wet soggy bandages on the floor. Donna came to the bathroom and consoled my broken self by helping me to clean my wounds and clean my dressing.

My life was never the same again. Trust was something that you earned, and I trusted no one. Everyone in my world was a threat, a potential threat, a perpetrator. I hated living, hated the home, hated everything and everyone. I was lonely, lost, and unloved. I just existed!

After a few months, when I no longer had to wear bandages and I was settled into Ambler Primary

School, I learned to get comfortable in my traumatic existence. I still had not been reunited with my family like my mum, aunts, uncles, nan, and grandad. My brother was still in Aylesbury.

I remember my class teacher, Ms Morgan, she showed me a lot of TLC and affection and even encouraged me to sing. So much so that it became a regular occurrence for me to sing in assembly, even to the delight of my headmaster Mr O Sullivan. I loved to sing. I could escape my world and escape to a safe place and feel better. I'd immerse myself in music, song melodies, sound, rhythm, and harmony. The bliss was real.

For the first time in my life, I made friends who were the same colour as me. Sandra used to come back to Elwood street with me, she was jovial, friendly, and caring. Her big sister used to come and pick us up sometimes, and we would stroll up Blackstock road together laughing and talking about everything and anything, except of course about my troubled life.

Then there was Brandy, a West Indian girl who resembled more of an Indian girl than a Caribbean one. I used to go to Brandy's house before school, pick her up, then we'd meet Sandra and have fun at school all day, it was great. Sandra later went on to join me at secondary school, Highbury Fields in September 1981. The highlight of our school life was netball. We loved it! She could shoot, like a champion. I played goal defence. We never lost a match either!

Warm Flames

We were sat by the fire in the front room, it was warm & cosy on an early spring evening. The atmosphere was laced with wandering smells of sherry and other alcoholic smells. As my aunt and I were on the floor by the fire she poured out her heart. Her pain hugged me, wrapping itself around my broken spirit. Misery does surely love company. Even though at the age of thirteen, I was too young to understand that saying, now I can see crystal clear what that actually means.

My aunt didn't have a clue what I had had to endure during my formative years as I didn't have the words to express the torture I suffered. I still hadn't cried for all the loss in my life. I was mute. I now understand why Maya Angelou cited in her autobiographical work, "I Know Why The Caged Bird Sings," that she too was mute following an assault that she experienced as a child.

I came to see the world as a dangerous place of twists and turns, valleys and gullies and no one could be trusted, by any means necessary.

Somehow, without me telling her what I endured, there was such a level of hurt, guilt and sorrow and empathy coming from her that she flooded the room with her pain and despair. We were there the entire evening and my aunt filled me in on what seemed like a lifetime of family history from when I was "stolen" by the social services during a nine-year gap of my life with tales about family. I listened to her cries and anguish into the early hours of the morning in front of the fire.

Funny how she mirrored my pain. I felt warm inside. She cared. Her voice echoed with sounds of crying, helpless and hopeless but at the same time the tone and pitch touched my soul with a long lost yearning for a love that I had craved for all my life. As she guzzled on her beer, it was as if she was medicating the hurt, grief and sorrow and anguish, guilt, and helplessness. The more she became intoxicated, it was as if it eased talking about the trauma of my brother and me that bit easier to bear.

One day when we were having this time together, I'd gone upstairs to have a chat with my two cousins. As I was coming downstairs to get something I heard my mum's voice, I was thinking "oh no" I bet she's been drinking too, my heart started to race. I remember thinking, she's going to ask me for money to get a beer, or ask me for cigarettes and start criticizing me for one reason or another. My aunt shouted up to me as I was coming down the stairs, "she's started again, she thinks I'm stealing you from her, she's accusing me of taking you away". So next thing you know I'm in the middle of an argument, but five minutes later it was all over.

It was a lovely summer day during the holidays and the music was blasting from my aunt's front room. Her good friend Bishop, a kind friendly man in his seventies, was showing off a record, a twelve-inch LP called Computer Love. At the time, that was 'thee song' of all anthems, it was an eighties classic. I was fascinated that a man, a pensioner, could be so with the times and in tune with the youth of our era. I mean he bought that song with his weekly allowance.

I used to go to my aunts' house at lunchtime, sometimes with my friends, from school, which was only a fifteen-minute walk away. At other times I'd go after school and spend the evening, and my aunt and I would finish where we left off with what I'd missed in my former years. One day, I finally got to hear her account about the truth behind my brothers near fatality and his long stay and rehabilitation at Great Ormond Street. She spoke of his severe life-altering and life-changing injuries. I had no words!

There was a glimmer of light in the darkness of living in a strange children's home in Highbury, and that was reacquainting myself with my family that was organized by Robert. I was told that my uncle Robert, who I'd never met before, would be coming to pick me up from Elwood street and that I'd be going to stay at my nan's house over Christmas. I was neither happy nor excited, just indifferent.

The day that Robert arrived I was ready, suitcase packed. I met him at the door. He was really big, looked strong and had a caring face. He didn't really smile but his turning up communicated to me that he cared. We didn't really know what to say, and I was only thirteen at the time. He was completely oblivious to what I had endured throughout my childhood and being mute from shock didn't help. I was beyond the expression of the painful feelings and thoughts of my harrowing childhood and felt unloved, rejected, abandoned, and neglected.

The smell of home at nan's house wrapped around me like a warm hug. The chicken was cooking in the duchee pot, yam, banana, dumpling, and choco were boiling in another pot, and a medley of other dishes created a concoction of home love that cuddled me. It felt good.

I didn't want to go back to Elwood street. My mind drifted to the God of heaven, maybe he was real? I mean I'd gone to Sunday school at the baptist church in Highbury fields and regularly attended since having come back to London from Hertfordshire but had not really had an encounter or experience with Him. Going to my nan's house for the first time was an experience. That Christmas was the best one ever, my family was huge, there were so many aunts and uncles and cousins and family friends. It was a nonstop party at nans. I was so at home.

One day Robert came to see me at Elwood street and told me that I was going to have a new social worker by the name of Corby Ward. I was indifferent at the time, but I remember the day she came and introduced herself to me about a month later. I had a feeling of comfort. There was something genuine about her, she seemed caring, humourous and took to me like a duck to water. She was motherly, and her frame housed her airy, jovial, larger than life character. Was she a real-life angel?. I felt so much light flooding the atmosphere with her exuberant, charismatic and radiant energy.

Corby spent a good hour with me on her first visit. I felt that I'd made a friend. She was a larger than life character, elegant, and sophisticated. She had golden hair that she'd pin up into a waterfall, wore lovely perfume and light lipstick and dressed with an air of class and sophistication. "It's been lovely meeting you and I'm looking forward to us doing some life story work together," she said before arranging to see me in two weeks time. I felt a warmth that I had never felt before, and I smiled.

Signs Towards The Light

I started secondary school shortly after that meeting and loved it. Corby phoned me after school one evening to say that she wanted to take me out at lunchtime during school one day to Jones Brothers. It was a big department store on Holloway road that had what I would call a posh restaurant. I smiled on the phone. "Shall I wait by the main gate at the school?" I said. She replied " when you come outside you'll see me waiting in my white mini metro" she responded, "Ok....see you Thursday".

Thursday couldn't come quick enough. I'd never had anyone take me out to lunch before. I woke up early that morning, it was a warm spring sunny day, the skyline promised hope of a new day, as the clouds floated beyond the blue sky I had an unusual light-hearted feeling in my spirit. This was a strange feeling, but it was somehow pleasant, although contrary to the feeling of heaviness and dread that I usually had when I woke up first thing.

As I gazed out of the window that day I couldn't contain myself. I got ready in record time, washed, dressed, breakfast in the blink of an eye and out the door. Coupled with the fact that I did actually like school, I loved it. I was the first one there that day. Miss Jarosz, my favourite teacher would be arriving soon. I loved that lady. We had an unspoken agreement since that day she showed so much compassion to me that I could go and see her any time of the day if I was feeling sad, which was all the time.

I knew her timetable better than she did and knew when she'd be in her small shared school office which happened to be the first aid area as well, that she shared with three or four other teachers.

She worked in PE, and we got it off from day one. Miss Jarosz was tall and athletic with brown eyes and olive-like skin. She looked Mediterranean but was from Poland. She was funny, friendly and wore a beige duffle coat that went with her worn sports bag and worn trainers, but she actually looked cool and sporty.

I couldn't concentrate in class that morning, I was unusually unsettled and was thinking about Corby coming at lunchtime, so much so that I walked out of my classroom like I often did and went to find Miss Jarosz. I needed to see someone that cared and wasn't going to ask me a hundred and one questions. I needed to see a friendly face and maybe even have a hot drink. I went to the staff room first and knocked on the door, but she wasn't there. So I went a long way round to her shared office on the ground floor, but I had a feeling she wouldn't be there on her own, so I took the long way round.

As I was walking down the corridor I heard the deep, hollow voice of Mrs Mann, the headteacher who appeared to have the frame of an imposing giant. Strangely enough, I never felt intimidated or scared, she was like a gentle giant. "Urrgh" her voice seemed to follow and find me down the corridor, "Is everything ok"? I turned around to see a reserved, smiling expression on her face, but one that showed sincere concern. " I'm alright, just looking for Miss Jarosz, have you seen her"?

"I think she might be in her office," "ok" I responded. I'll go and see if she's there. "Alright," she said. So I went to the office, knocked on the door, another teacher answered the door, and as she did she said hello, "is Miss Jarosz there"? "Sorry not at the moment, she's teaching but will be back in shortly, you can wait here for her if you want?" "Ok," I said and sat in the area outside her office. She strolled in the office and gave me a smile and said in her light humour she chuckled as if she enjoyed being there for me, "what are you doing here with a big smile on her face, shall we go into the other room?"

As if she knew my answer my response would be as if she understood the code that if I was waiting for her then I wanted to see her in private. "I'll get the key," and within seconds we were going to a nice cosy little room that we sometimes went to if her shared office was occupied. This room was opposite the main entrance of the school entrance, with glass-paned doors that open out onto the reception but provided privacy if needed.

So we went in, I sat in front of the desk and leaned my head on the desk of my folded arms. She sat a foot or two near me with her hands relaxed in her lap, we just had some quiet time. I don't recall saying anything other than I can't concentrate in class. She understood but wanted to know what was unsettling me today.

"Corby's coming to take me out at lunchtime". "Oh, that's nice," she responded." But I had mixed feelings, no one had ever given me special attention before, could she be trusted. I knew that she had struck a chord with me on our first meeting and I sensed she was ok, that she wasn't a baddie, but at the same time I struggled with conflicting feelings around mistrust, abandonment, abuse, and manipulation. All these contradictory emotions meddled with the pending excitement of going out for a treat.

At eleven years old, my feelings were beyond articulation but were played out in school, which I can honestly say that as a child was the safest place for me to be.

We spent about ten minutes together before the school bell went for a break, so I said goodbye, "have a nice time" Miss Jarosz smiled and winked at me, the fear disappeared for the rest of the morning.

It was lunchtime, and I left the class five minutes earlier than usual, I went to wait outside, and Corby's car was actually there, and there she was sitting with the passenger window seat half-open. I went to open the door to a warm, jovial welcome, we smiled at each other. "You look nice, she said," I blushed, I was shy and not used to compliments, and they made me feel self-conscious.

At the same time, I felt special with Corby, and we took a liking to each other. Lunch was fun, we actually ended up going to McDonald's in the end, I felt like the most special girl in the whole wide world. My friends at school were eating canteen food, and here I was with my newfound 'nice friend' driving in her cute car and eating at McD's. Smiling + Safe.

As she drove me back to school, I was looking forward to seeing her again. This time she was going to come to Elwood street, and we were going to do life story work. What was that about?

It was a weekday evening and I was at my so-called home waiting by the window eagerly anticipating Corby's arrival. She arrived a little bit early. When I went to the door I was greeted by a huge warm jovial spirited smile that shone through my brokenness. She had an aura of light that was comforting and angelic that somehow made me feel secure and safe. An odd feeling that I wasn't accustomed to the feeling, given the fact that I had by this point, survived the nearness of death!

My world lit up, I felt happy that I would be in the company of this lovely lady and have her undivided attention. I had an odd but warm feeling. I had never experienced anyone giving me the time of day much less having one to one with someone special. Hope felt strange, I understood the term 'duck out of water.'

She came into the house, and we went into the lounge and dining room and sat at a table where we as kids usually did our homework or played games like scrabble or connect four. Corby radiated a compassionate caring heart. She was warm and bright, we talked about school, my hobbies and what I enjoyed reading. I spoke about a book that I was reading called The Famous Five and spoke about some of the poems I had written.

This initial meeting was to mark the beginning of a seven-year relationship between an angel and me. It was usual for Corby to come and meet me in her white mini metro at Highbury Fields school, regularly. At least every other week. She'd take me to either McDonalds for lunch which was a great treat, or we'd go to Jones Brothers on Holloway Road in Islington and have lunch there, what I would call their posh restaurant.

Sometimes, Miss Jarosz would come with us too. We'd talk about school, or Elwood street or my brother who I was estranged from. I developed a strong bond with Corby, and we'd write letters and poems to each other. Looking back I realize that God had used her to tap into my creative genius as a way to resurrect the deeply buried trauma, hurt, and pain that had become buried beneath layers of guilt and fear. She had bought me the first special book that I would write some of my poems in. I remember my first poem started like "there's a hole in my heart; you can fill it for me if you lived my life, you'd be able to see."

The night that I wrote that poem, I remember I came in from school, feeling so sad and alone. I went to my bedroom that I shared with Jaqueline and Donna, but they weren't in at the time. So I got out my book and poured out all my hurt and pain that were scribed through my torn and aching soul. Each letter that was articulated through the ink bled into words of sorrow and separation, loss and abandonment.

When I finished writing I took my poem downstairs to Jean. She was one of the social workers that worked in the home and were on duty that day. She was sitting in her favourite chair by the fire with her dog Holly. I showed her my poem but don't recall her saying anything, but her face looked sallow as if life was ebbing out of her. She looked like a human shock absorber as if she had absorbed all the trauma that had split onto the lined paper in the book. I left the room with my book in hand, feeling as if I had released some of the burdens and went to bed.

Corby was arranging to take me to a country cottage to do some life story work, and I was in for a big treat. I remember the evening that she called me to say that she was going to pop round in a couple of days to tell me all about it. I was so excited. I'd never gone away before, so it was a BIG thing.

When Corby told me all about it, I became even more excited at all the facilities, an open fire in the lounge, a sauna, swimming pool, trouser press and kettle in the room, etc. You might be thinking what is so exciting about some of that? Well at the age of thirteen I was a tomboy, so the thought of me being able to put my waffles (boys trousers that were the in thing in the eighties) was like playing with grown-up toys.

We drove down to this cottage type of hotel that was buried in the country somewhere. We got there late afternoon and settled in. All I can remember was sitting in this cosy lounge on a chesterfield that was in front of this vast open country fireplace. We talked about lots of things, living with the Hamilton's in Hoddesdon Hertfordshire, being separated from Richard, my close relationship with Miss Jarosz and lots of other things.

The warm roaring fire melted away at my afflicted soul and nursed the wounds of a childhood endured. For the first time in my life I was around somebody heartfelt, friendly, and I felt safe, I felt protected, and I was free to express myself through the loyal caring and supportive friendship and the activated gift of poetry. I found my voice!

Thinking about it now, when the bible talks about entertaining angels amongst strangers, I can thank the

Lord that He has kept me to testify of seeing the scriptures come alive. Corby was an angel sent to me from heaven, and she contributed my creative gift of poetry which would later lead to songwriting, then singing and acting, dancing and a love of the arts that I would fully come to get involved in as my life unfolded.

Along with this bond came the fear of loss. Was this friendship with Corby going to last? What if something happened to her? My anxieties were based on my earlier losses, but as a child, I was unable to process my thoughts, and at times it all seemed a bit too much. After all, was I really worth loving I would question?

I'd more or less died inside at a very young age, I'd say from about seven years old when my innocence was stolen. I was unable to tell anyone about what I'd endured because the shame was unbearable, and my violated body could barely cope with the trapped and hidden trauma.

So, on the one hand, I was cultivating a secure attachment for the first time of my life with this woman who loved me from the heart. I mean it. There were things that she did for me beyond the call of duty which I'll talk about later!

There was a real dilemma I had and that was based on trust. Was it ok to let you in? To hope again and dare to experience laughter and joy, after all, I was alienated from those feelings through my childhood.

Help! Where do I go and who would I turn to? My childhood illustrated to me that perpetrators of abuse projected their pathology onto innocent victims. That the exploited, due to their vulnerability, had no means of protection or escape. This trust thing was a HUGE risk, but somehow, it was as if I had discerned that

Corby was not only ok but that she was right for me. It was as if her heart was tangible through the loving, tentative, and comforting acts of kindness.

To trust meant that I'd be faced with the fear of rejection, abandonment, pain, and abuse. Maybe another near encounter of the iron clutches of racism or near death that I was so familiar with when I was estranged from the very thing that I needed most. But, you see, I knew Corby's love for me was real, she wasn't just a social worker, she was my buddy, my friend, a safe person who was warm and kind.

The poems she used to write to me that tapped into my hidden genius and allowed me to express my aching, bruised, delicate, and fragile soul. She cradled my hurt with such grace, love, and dignity. The acts of love by taking me away to stay at her house with her daughter to escape the cold institution of a childcare system that was devoid of the essence of family.

The makeup that she bought me were tiny pots of loose eyeshadow that resembled differing hues of copper, gold, cinnamon, and sun-kissed cocoa that had fallen from the sun that I'd use as makeup to adorn my skin. This was hand made bespoke high end make up.

For five years, Corby and I had built a kind, compassionate, and loving relationship. I was really close to her, she was my light in the dark. I was sixteen by now, and I was hearing talk going around at Elwood Street and me moving onto a hostel in Highbury New Park. I felt indifferent.

One day Corby and I were in McDonald's, and she asked me about school and had seen Miss Jarosz recently. I walked out of maths and went to see her today, and we spoke about the end of the year sports day. "Are you going to do your hundred meters like last year because you won last year didn't you if I remember well?" she said. I smiled as if winning was something alien! "Yea, I might do, I'm not sure yet."

She smiled. "You know that you're outgrowing living at Elwood street," she said, "I mean before you know it you'll be seventeen years old". I was thinking to myself, I only just turned sixteen, how come we're looking at the year ahead? The words were unable to come out, I sensed a pending threat. I didn't know what to say.

I sensed a change was on the horizon. I'd gotten used to the people who cared for me like Rosalyn, a joyous lady and Steve. When they worked on shift together it was as if they became a dancing duo. Their actions, words, thoughts, and deeds were in synergy. They laughed, played around, joked and cooked up the best tasty food together. We'd go out on day trips in the summer to Margate and literally be rolling over ourselves with laughter. I was becoming hardened to life, though. The pain sometimes that I felt as a child was so intense. I mean, my mum wasn't around she was struggling through the torture of having her children taken away. The only way she survived was through the intoxicating concoction of the most potent beer you could imagine. Her life revolved around medicating the pain.

When Corby would ask me about my mum instead of bursting into tears from feeling rejected and abandoned, I'd bottle up my emotion, and the only way to express my hurt was through a frown. I became used to the agony of being separated from my family, I had lost touch with George, my dad from the age of four, Richard and I were biologically related but only in that sense.

It wouldn't be until I was twenty-eight and accepted the Lord Jesus Christ as my saviour that the Lord would use a preacher of the gospel to reveal to me that it was good to be afflicted so that I could learn His ways. That what the devil meant for the evil God would turn it around for my good. The Lord would use the enemy to be a footstool. That when my mother and father forsake me that the Lord would take me up. Psalms 27 was a poignant scripture for me.

"1. The Lord is my light and my salvation; whom shall I fear The Lord is the stronghold of my life; Of whom shall I be afraid? 2. When evildoers assail me to eat up my flesh, my adversaries and foes, it is they who stumble and fall 3. Though an army encamp against me, my heart shall not fear; though war arise against me yet I will be confident. 4. One thing I have asked of the Lord that I will seek after that I may dwell in the house of the Lord all the days of my life, to gaze upon the beauty of the Lord & to inquire in His temple. 5. He will hide me in a shelter in the array of trouble; he will conceal me under cover of His tent He will lift me high upon a rock 6. And now my head shall be lifted up above my enemies all around me, and I will offer in His tent sacrifices with shouts of joy; I will sing and make melody to The Lord".

In later years It would come to be a sovereign word that girded me up. It underpinned my very existence, was my foundation and became something that I could testify about. It wouldn't be until nearly two decades later that I'd be crying out to the Lord and thanking Him for saving me from the clutches of death at the age of sixteen and surviving the agonizing departure of my dear friend Corby who invested so much love, time, compassion and beauty into my life.

As salvation was about to come, The Lord was preparing me in advance for one of the worst tragedies that would come the following year. At the same time, it then meant I could hold my head up from the shame of having an alcoholic mother.

Salvation

He uses the foolish things to confound the wise. 1 Corinthians 1:27

1997 was a significant year for me on lots of fronts. Good things were happening, I was enjoying working with children in care and was based at a children's home in Tooting, south London. When I look back I see how God had used the anguish of my childhood to reach out and care for other neglected children.

I smile because the Lord used the past as a key for my vocation and now calling. It all testifies to the love I had for children that I worked within the care system. I understood the challenging behaviour of the children. I totally got it! I had been there. I was able to empower and influence the children to be the best that they could be when they were at their most vulnerable, and I loved it.

The home in Tooting was very similar to Elwood street where I went into care after my foster placement broke down in 1980. The main difference was that there were African and Caribbean children and black staff. I more or less run that home in Tooting.

I took it for granted at the time, but I used to have complete responsibility for three to four teenagers in this four-bedroom house. I was about twenty-six at the time. I got on well with the staff that I worked with amazingly well with the children too.

In particular, I met a girl about my age who worked there as well. Her name was Charlotte. I liked her independence and the fact that she travelled to America a lot, I even began to go to places like Virginia in the USA with her which was so amazing. I remember I was involved in a lot of singing projects when I worked in Tooting and it was normal for me to finish a sleep in which would typically start at two in the afternoon until 11 pm at night. I'd then sign off at eleven in the evening, sleep there overnight in the snug room that they had for staff, then start shift at seven in the morning and finish at three in the afternoon.

Often, I'd go home for a couple of hours and I'd either be singing out at an event or I'd be in the studio or working with a band that I was in called Freestyle. One day all the children and staff came to see me sing at Hackney Empire. They were all sitting right in the front, I could see their faces light up amongst the thousands of people that were there who I couldn't really see beyond the glaring stage lights.

I sang a song called God Bless the Child, and everyone loved it. The children and staff were amazed, it was such a lovely experience, the joy from colleagues, friends, children, and the wider audience warmed me inside. Life in moments like that felt like a dream. As a strong lead singer and holding my own, I felt appreciated, accepted, loved and could shine through expressing my voice, I loved it.

One day when Charlotte and I had the weekend off work, she took me to a church that was holding its services in a place called The Brix. She wasn't a Christian herself, but I knew she was searching for something more in life, so I happily tagged along. We went into this room that resembled a roman theatre. The seating was like a semi-circle that started from a central podium where praise and worship was, and the choir singers and the accommodation ascended from the ground up.

So we enter this room from the seats at the top to the smoke of divine praise and worship. People were crying, making loads of noise, some were bowed over, the atmosphere was tangible with this beautiful presence which I came to learn was the Holy Ghost.

I could see the pastor that I recognized from a gospel show that was aired in the eighties on television. He was wearing a purple regal suit and stood out from the crowd. There was something different about this man, I was fascinated. I don't recall him preaching because people were wailing on the floor and screaming, there were church workers caring for them.

I came to later understand that extravagant worship could cause healing and deliverance. Charlotte and I managed to ease and squeeze ourselves into one of the seats at the top, and as I sat down, I remembered encounters that I'd had with the Holy Spirit when I listened to people like Lavine Hudson and Take Six and went to concerts to see Ann Nesby from the Sounds of Blackness.

I wanted His presence, I wanted God, and I was the first to run to the podium to receive the Lord in my heart and confess my sins, say the sinners prayer and start my new journey as a baby in Christ. I was elated for days and weeks after that God encounter. I had a huge spring in my step, I felt light-hearted, His presence was beautiful. I used to go and worship on the common when church used to be outside of the building and listen to one of the pastors during praise and worship which would cause me to fall out on the grass from being overwhelmed with the power of God.

It was during this season that God started to use people to reveal the many facets of love, agape and eros love to name but some.

Rosa was a friend that I'd met on the art scene and one of the many friends that used to come and support me when I was singing. She was a tall Nigerian young woman from a strong close-knitted family. She was made with the most caring genes inscribed in her DNA, and although I never spoke about my hidden pain, her spirit flowed like a river of deep compassion that would refresh and revive my soul that sometimes bowed down in grief like a weeping willow tree that gravitated to the brook.

She once gave me a poem that she had framed and laminated and wrapped in ribbons that read:

Love

Ultimately love is self-approval.
Love is placed you are coming from, your ground of being.
You are love

Love is the divine force everywhere, the universal energy, the moving power of life that flows in your own heart

Love is accepting someone as he and she is or as he or she is not

Love is the acknowledgement of a union that already exists

You are already part of this unifying essence called love. In addition, you are either loving or not loving. If you are caring, people will feel this attractive force and will appear in your path so you can love them. And there are multitudes of people who want to express their love to you. It is important to realize, however, that you cannot accept anyone more than you are willing to give to yourself. Self-love, many people have had so much disapproval, they have forgotten how to go about loving themselves. What is self-love?

Self- love is acknowledging and praising yourself verbally to yourself.

Self -love is approving of all your actions

Self- love is having confidence in your ability

Self- love is giving yourself pleasure without guilt

Self- love is loving your body and admiring your beauty

Self- love is giving yourself what you want and feeling you deserve it

Self- love is letting yourself win

Self- love is letting others in instead of submitting yourself to loneliness

Self- love is following your own tuition

Self-love is making your own rules responsibly

Self-love is seeing your own perfection

Self- Love is taking credit for what you did

Self-love is surrounding yourself with beauty

Self-love is letting yourself be rich and not staying in Poverty

Self-love is creating an abundance of friends

Self-love is rewarding yourself and never punishing yourself

self -love is trusting yourself

Self-love is nourishing yourself with good food and good ideas

Self-love is surrounding yourself with people who sustain you

Self-love is forgiving yourself

Self-love is treating yourself equal to others

Self-love is letting in affection

Self-love is developing your creative ideas

Self-love is having fun all the time

Self-love is really talking to yourself gently and loving

Self-love is becoming your own approving parent

Self-love is turning all your negative thoughts to affirmations

Rosa concluded by saying to me that there are lots of people who can be friendly, but it takes someone like you to be a true friend.

She turned out to be a loyal sister that stood by me through thick and thin. There's a saying that says people come into your life for a reason, a season or a lifetime. The reason Rosa was in my life during one of the most significant seasons of my life was to show me that life wasn't always cruel, that it had a way of giving you special gifts that sometimes resemble people with loving hearts and selflessness. God's supreme love was so overwhelming though. It's an overarching all-encompassing love. It's this love that has kept me alive, supernaturally.

Weeping May Endure For A Night

"Lord, I just don't understand, I've been in this choir now for nearly four years, the day I joined I knew that I was in the right place, after all, singing was something that I had done all my life. I'm here with all these choir angels, we're all on one accord, or so it seemed, and this joy I'm experiencing can only come from you because you are God alone". This became my dialogue with HIm. My experience of being in the choir ministry was initially joyful and fulfilling. It was what I was born to do. I loved it! Over time God began to bless me with Christian brothers and sisters who became the family I never had. We'd all go out for lunch after ministering in song all morning on Sunday in the choir. They'd be up to eight of us sometimes, and we'd go to a nice restaurant and fellowship for the afternoon until it was time to go back to the minister for the evening service.

I felt like part of the family which was something that I had not experienced as a child, so this was a big thing to me. My aunt was also in the choir, but she would literally run out of the church after ministering in the choir. Something had drastically changed between us but I couldn't put my finger on it. All I knew was that something was wrong, very wrong!

I brought her to my then church in 1998 following the death of my late mother. When I joined the choir in 2009, although at first, my aunt was pleasant towards me, gradually this changed. Favour sometimes is not fair, may late grandmother had given me a gift which I have come to learn, as it was with Joseph in the bible suffered because his father favoured him, so it was with me at this time.

She didn't want to sit next to me, didn't want to travel home together, she wasn't interested in talking about nan and became hostile, cold and bitter, for what reason I didn't know. One thing was for sure that hate didn't come from God.

The word says in 1 John 4:20 "whoever claims to love God yet hates his brother or sister is a liar. For whoever does not love their brother and sister, whom they have seen, cannot love God, whom they have not seen".

I could see that divisive forces were angry at the prospect of us being truly united in the spirit of love and togetherness. Uniting in love with my blood relatives became challenging and opposing forces of love were blocking any unity among us. I said to God, You loved me SO Much that you died for me. Yes, just for me so that I would not die but have everlasting life. 1 Peter 2:24

The real issue here is that there is a war going on between heaven and hell. The bible says, "how good and how pleasant it is for us to dwell in unity". Psalms 113:1. Despite the enemy trying to create a divide, we know God is into families.

Well, I'd say by being ignored and overlooked it was as if I was fighting a spirit of disunity and the enemy was trying to block me. It was a case of putting everything in God's hands and letting God go before me to deal with the enemy of disunity and contention.

David in the bible was a reject, Jesus Himself was rejected as was Joseph by his own flesh and blood. Then look at the orphan Esther. Well the Lord said that the stone that the builder rejected became the CHIEF cornerstone. Psalms 118:22. He would cause the devil to work for me and be my foot stall. Things were about to take a turn and I was about to see God's mighty hand at work.

He Called Me Candy

It's the seventh of April 2013 and I am sitting in the Miracle Healing Service. I'd arranged to sit with Sarah. I'd met her four years before at church. On that day back then the Lord had me outside the sanctuary in the faith reception on my own, and this was really unusual. After ministering in the choir with my sisters, we'd often go out for lunch together, but the Lord had different plans that day.

I sat by the church bookshop for a bit wondering why the Lord had secluded me as He did. I looked over to my right from the bench in the foyer to see Sarah perched on the enclave between the information desk and the stairs to the office upstairs and said hi, how you doing? "Yeah, I'm ok" Sarah replied, her face showing that she wasn't alright. Sarah was in her mid-twenties her hair was short and natural and she wore in twists, she had a nice brown honey tone to her skin and was a small to medium build.

At that moment when Sarah responded to me, her glow was no longer there, her eyes were sullen, her usual ripe cheeks had no colour, and her shoulders were hunched over as if she was bowed down in grief. I walked over to her and said, "Sarah, what's wrong?" She opened up to me and shared what had been going on.

In short, I spent three hours ministering to her that day and telling her how special she was. That she was loved and cherished and wanted and that Jesus died especially for her so that Sarah wouldn't have to bear the pain of what she had experienced in her traumatic childhood.

I shared my testimony with her, how God had snatched me out of the hands of the enemy, that if it was not for Him I would have been dead like the tragic death of Victoria Climbe who died at the abuse of her carers. I told her about the pain of having an alcoholic mother as she had an alcoholic mother who used to drink with all the drunkards outside the main gate in Finsbury Park.

I said that as a child I carried a lot of shame, low self-esteem, weak confidence, and rejection. But when I got saved in 1997 He redeemed me from the curse of Satan. I spoke Jeremiah 1:5 that before she was formed in her mother's womb that He knew her. I shared that the Lord gave me a church home six months before my mum died, that as tragic as it was to lose my mother at such a young age that if it was not for the Lord, I might have taken my life as well, but shared that He is a good God.

This was the first time in my Christian life, I had the opportunity to experience what my then pastor always preached about. He always said that the challenges you go through in life are what gives you information for your future. That you overcome by the blood of the lamb and the word of your testimony Rev 12:11 KJV

What was unusual about this experience was that I got to see the fruit of sharing my testimony and how by encouraging others with the word of God and kind words can build people up and impact them in such a way that it could alter people's life.

Three years later, when I was getting ready to minister in the choir, I saw Sarah with three other dancers getting ready to worship through dance. I was so elated that day and so thankful to God as to what He was doing in her life. He did promise that what you sow in tears you would reap in joy (Psalms 126:5 KJV).

It wouldn't be until four years later, on one of the sunniest springs days of the year on Saturday the sixth of April that I met up properly with Sarah again. We'd often see each other in passing, we would greet each other with a warm smile and go on our way. She had said to me a few months back in the autumn of the year before that she wanted to have a chat, that there has been a lot of good things happening. But I discerned that there were things going on that were communicated to me through her tone of voice and weary eyes.

I was looking forward to the day when that would happen, well, if God willed it and so he did on a weekend it became one of the poignant eras of my life. In fact, it was only a few weeks ago at the Prophetic Praise and Prayer conference that Sarah approached me at the end of the evening sessions asking to borrow my phone to call a cab to church. God used our brief encounters to set the scene, the backdrop if you like to hasten and perform His word, Jerimiah 1:12, immediately and suddenly.

We were sitting in Nando's in a cosy corner of the restaurant. I felt privileged to sit next to a young woman of God who was so changed from the girl that I met in the faith reception at church years before.

The hue of her skin tone resembled a warm, caramel palate mixed with honey. She had an inner radiance that could not entirely be created with makeup. She was radiant, her brown eyes glimmered with secrets that someone special like Jesus had shared with her. I could see she had had an encounter with God that had changed her life. Her brown velvet twists were swept off her face with a yellow band, and they hung like small bobbled strings of cocoa beads that gave her a country girl look who was raised on a Caribbean farm.

I admired the God in her, and her presence ushered in a level of service from the waiting staff only deserving of royalty. At least four different people approached us within a few minutes of us sitting down. I said her to beware of entertaining angels amongst strangers. The expression that I got was one that said, "I'm meek, lowly, and humble" and mixed with "I'm undeserving." I thought at that moment that Sarah was being transformed into his image but with childlike innocence or maybe even lack awareness of how blessed she really was.

As we sat there, I said that it's charming to have fellowship and that I was looking forward to hearing how she'd been getting on. "Patrice, even though the ministry that I joined isn't exactly the dream in my heart, God has just blessed me so much," I smiled and bore witness to the favour and blessings on her life. "A lot has gone on at church," she said with a tired expression.

For the next hour or two, I listened intently to the humiliation she had experienced from her team leader and sisters in ministry. The rejection and pain she went through just to serve the Lord, the lies that had been told to Bishop about her from her sister in the ministry she was in, and I so emphasized with what she said.

Little did she know that I could so relate to what she said, I had personally found that I had worse treatment from Christians in the church than in the world. That I too, was in a season of discouragement, had been feeling rejected, isolated, overlooked and left on the backside corner of the desert. I didn't share this with Sarah as I discerned that she was feeling ignored. The beautiful thing about Sarah's story was that there was a fantastic testimony to come, which for me allowed me to see the word in action. That the stone that the builder rejected became the chief cornerstone (Psalms 118:22) and He said that He will make your enemies be afoot stalled (Luke 20:43).

The very people that she worked with within the church caused her a lot of oppression, heartache, and sadness, the Lord turned it around so that He promoted her as a dance teacher and leader in two churches near where she lived. She had the full support of the reverend who requested that she teach young children to dance in ministry.

I was so overjoyed for her. She was celebrated, accepted, valued, and given authority to run her own department outside of the church to which she belonged. The beautiful thing about her testimony was that I admired her charm. Yes, she had every right to be bitter, but God had made her better and as far as I could see she was not only loving her enemies by keeping her peace, but she continued to sit under her leader which I admire as a real act of humility.

After having listened intently for some time and enjoying doing so, Sarah said, "Patrice, I've been doing all the talking, you haven't said anything about you yet". I smiled big, knowing that sowing the fruit listening was more powerful than talking. I responded by saying, "I just wanted to give you the time to talk about yourself and let you flow". Her expression told me by the warm flash of perfect set teeth and cheeks that left shiny impressions of rosy red apples that I had struck a chord.

I also sensed that she wanted to listen too, so I spoke of my passion for writing and the projects that I was currently working on, and as I was sharing I could see that she became inspired and she just started speaking words of life. She said, "Patrice, I just believe that God is doing great work in your life, that He notices you, He sees you and that He really cares about you. I see that through the calling and ministry that is in you that you will nurse children at your breasts. God is going to do amazing things in your life. I see you going to America, that God is going to do something great for you. You will get married and have children.

She was just flowing and speaking to me from her spirit. I thanked her for sharing with me but said that God had not shown me America. She was cool with what I said. I also think that because I got a postcard from Jesus at Ellel ministries a few months earlier, I really felt that God was calling me to finally get delivered, healed, restored and equipped to minister at a residential bible school. I mean He couldn't have given me a more definite sign and location, but He was also showing me the generous side to HIs nature in the next few days which was just amazing.

Little did I know that God had some major plans for me that weekend and that on the following day at church at the evening service, the husband and wife who were both pastoring my former church were about to confirm God's word over my life. To go to America where I was going to walk in the manifestation of my God-ordained new name Candy.

A name called out over me that meant I was entering into a sweet place of blessings, angels, honey, and all things lovely.

So after Sarah had spoken about America, it looked like the spirit wanted to take over, and I started to speak words of life to her, so much so that she began to ask me to pray for specific things in her life which I happily did. She was hungry for the Holy Spirit and so wanted to see the manifestation of the promises of God over her life. I was more than happy to speak the word of God concerning victory. She was elated. The funny thing was, although when we got to Nando's, there was hardly anyone there. Throughout our time there, loads of children came in for a birthday party. I mean a BIG kiddies celebration. I think that because we prayed and invited the holy spirit when we got there all the jovial noise didn't bother us at all. Jesus was in that fellowship and the presence of His peace and joy gave us contentment.

Sarah and I are at the 6pm service with her daughter. a beautiful girl with a cascade of bouncy shoulder-length honey-golden loose curls. She looked like a fair Caribbean version of Shirley Temple, she was about eight years old and huddled along with several other young toddlers and kids. Don't get me wrong I love children, but there was so much chaos in that row I literally could not sit there with Sarah and the kids.

Other mums were up and down, some getting up to leave to the ladies or talk to other members of the church, others were making their way back to their seats and needed to bypass me to get to their row on the seat where they were sitting. The praise and worship were beautiful, but I just couldn't get to that place of true worship with so much distraction going on.

Sarah was in the aisle giving extravagant worship unto the Lord. She had asked me about ten minutes ago if I wouldn't mind looking after her daughter when she goes to the altar to dance. At the time I said I was more than happy to, but I got her attention a while after and I apologised to her.

"Sweetheart, I'm really sorry but I am going to sit somewhere else when you come back from dancing at the altar, it' just that there is so much distraction going on". Sarah lost the chubbiness from smiling in her cheeks, and her eyes dimmed with disappointment. I felt sorry that I had hurt her feelings, but I really needed to be in a place with God.

I managed to sit to the far left and a few rows in front to where I was sitting next to a lovely girl with a radiant smile and happy spirit. She was jovial, and I knew God had strategically placed me there. But then as I was praising God this woman just slipped herself between her and me, but I discerned she was troubled, I saw hostility and anger.

As the worship ended under the instruction from the man of God was for us to sit down. I kindly asked the lady if she would allow my sister to sit next to me and for us to exchange seats, but she just responded by a stern look on her face with coldness etched deep into the pores of her being. I wouldn't have minded so much if she wanted to talk to me but every time the bishop said, "turn to your neighbour and decree a blessing", she just refused to participate.

I was adamant that no one was going to steal my joy or blessing and asked the usher behind me to come into agreement with me which she gracefully and happily did. God just moved the distraction in His own special way.

Anyway about an hour or so later the man of God asked his wife who was the co-pastor to join him on the pulpit. She called out a sister's name and said the spirit of God was resting on her and spoke some incredible blessings into her life. Then she turned over to the right of the church where I was standing and looking over at me said, "is that Candy?" She was pointing at me, well I just looked behind me as Candy didn't bear witness to my spirit. Nevertheless, it turned out that she had zoned right in on me and said that I must come to the altar.

I was quite a way from the pulpit where she was standing a right fifteen rows or so in front of her. The church was packed out that night and as I made my way to the front where the pastor's wife was standing loads of people got up from their chairs to make room for me. As I approached the altar, I looked up at the pastor's wife standing at the top of the six stairs in front of me. I was intrigued, I was thinking Candy, Lord what is all this about I don't even have anyone in my family named Candy.

I looked at her, whenever I looked at her I always saw gold in the spirit, this occasion was no different. There was a beautiful soft light radiating from her, her aura glowed with the love of God. Although I had been in the church for several years I was becoming so discouraged with one thing or another. Now, The Lord had hand picked me out of a huge gathering of several hundred people to release a public blessing over my life.

The man of God seemed in awe of what God was saying to me through his wife. I was face to face with the beauty of the Lord and absorbed every precious moment that the Lord was lavishing on me. He was speaking through His servant to me as I was the apple of His eye.

Psalms 17:8 "Keep me as the apple of your eye; hide me in the shadow of your wings".

She asked me if Candy meant anything to me. I was puzzled as I couldn't immediately recollect that it did.

She said that I have been carrying a lot of bitterness but that if I don't let it go, it will destroy me. I was trembling inside because only God himself would know what I was going through.

She said God is giving me a new name. She prayed into my life that the bitterness would break straight away then her husband, the man of God interjected. He noted that Candy is the American term for sweets and that I would be going on a trip to America and that while I am over there that I would be completely set free from bitterness and walk into a sweet place and that something special was going to happen out there.

It was incredible to not only see that word come to pass with the confirmation through the prophecy I got the day before from Sarah but, amazing how God moved in the days that followed after.

That evening my life changed, I had such joy in my heart, I kept laughing inside and many people that witnessed my open prophecy began calling me by my new God name.

Everyone started calling me Candy, it felt amazing. They were saying things like can I come to America with you and others were smiling at me. I was overjoyed. My heart smiled from my spirit, and I was in awe. God revealed my new name for His glory, which is the sweetness of Him.

When God changed my name, a war was waged against the prophecy of what He had spoken. However, I fight from victory and not for it. Since 2013, when I first started to write this book over six years ago, the battle has been raging although by His grace, I continue to fight. His word remains the same and changes not. "Heaven and earth shall pass away, but my words by no means shall pass away" (Mathew 24:35).

I can consistently testify that I have seen the goodness of the Lord in the land of the living Psalm 27:13, regardless of my circumstances because God is above the earth and my umbilical cord remains connected to Him from now until eternity.

Old things have indeed passed away, and all things have become new (2 Corinthians 5:17).

The following scriptures are a constant reminder of the beautiful sweet name He has given me. Once again, the blessing of not giving up, after all, has been for me to experience His eternal blessings. I can truly serve others now from the right place other than an anguished one.

Psalm 34:8 Taste and see that the Lord is good; blessed is the man that takes refuge in Him

Psalm 119:103 How sweet are thy words unto my taste! yea, sweeter than honey to my mouth

Psalm 104:34 My meditation of Him shall be sweet: I will be glad in The Lord

So back to the journey home from church the evening that God changed my name, I got the train home with my choir sister, Rose, and all she kept saying was Candy and laughing and smiling and I even felt that the Lord was saying that He might want that name to be the title of this book!

When I got home I received a text message from an elder, Sharon, from my church who I warmed to very much. The message read, "I was so elated to hear prophesy over your life by the leading of the Lord. God has listened to your heart and O what a blessing He is bestowing on you. You are a wonderful woman of God". Eld Sharon.

About two weeks before, Just before our Prophetic, Prayer and Praise conference, she sent me a beautiful scripture from Isaiah 62:2.

For Zion's sake will I not hold my peace, and for Jerusalem's sake, I will not rest, until the righteousness thereof goes forth as brightness and the salvation thereof as a lamp that burneth. And the Gentiles shall see thy righteousness, and all the kings thy glory: and thou shall be called a new name, which the mouth of the Lord shall name. Though shalt also be called a crown of beauty in the hand of the Lord. And a royal diadem in the hand of thy God. Thou shall no more be termed forsaken; neither shall thy land be termed desolate: but thou shalt be called Hepzibah, and thy land Beaulah: for the Lord delighteth in thee, and thy land shall be married. For as a young man marrieth a virgin, so shall thy sons marry thee: and as thy bridegroom rejoiceth over the bride, so shall thy God rejoiceth over thee. I have set watchmen upon thy wall. O Jerusalem, which shall never hold their peace day or night: ye that make mention of the Lord, keep not silence, And give him no rest, till He establishes, and till he makes Jerusalem a praise in the earth. The Lord has sworn by HIs right hand, and by the arm of His strength, Surely I will no more give corn to be meat for thine enemies; and the sons of the stranger shall not drink thy wine, for which thou has labored: But they that have gathered it shall eat it, and praise the Lord; and they shall have bought it together shall drink it in the courts of my holiness. Go through, go through the gates; prepare ye the way of the people; cast up, cast up the highway; gather out the stones, lift up a standard for the people. Behold, the Lord hath proclaimed unto the end of the world, say ye to the daughter of Zion, Behold, thy salvation cometh: behold, his reward is with him, and his work before him. And they shall call them, The Holy People, The Redeemed of the Lord: and thou shall be called, Sought out. A city not forsaken the Lord.

As I read over this scripture that elder Sharon had sent me, I thought wow, Lord you really are hastening over your word to perform it, in other words, you really desire for the word to come to pass and are in a hurry. This scripture not only ministered to my spirit but spoke volumes about the God encounter that I had the night of my prophecy. He was saying to me that I will no longer be forgotten and desolate and that He was giving me a new name and that He delighteth in me as a daughter of Zion.

The Lord spoke through Sarah again the day after my special God encounter who spoke about her fantastic encounter in California at Bethel Church in Redding. I was thinking as she was talking to me, ok Lord, are you giving me a sign? Sara's words were, " I had an amazing time in 2011, I went there twice in one year, Bethel is a church based on Jesus Christ, their emphasis is on extravagant worship with an amazing culture of honour. No disrespect to our church here in London, but I was loved back from pain to manifesting the joy of the Lord. I mean, the way that everyone just loves on you, they're very expressive, it's not a 'religious' church".

I got what she meant, they loved the Lord so much and were so expressive in the way that everyone interacted, that protocol literally went out the door when it came to experiencing healthy and whole relationships and most of all the love of God.

I knew that Sarah was in a different place from when I first met her in 2009. I could see that although she felt unrecognised in church, overlooked and neglected by the church, God had moved in her life in a powerful way when she was at Bethel. When Sarah spoke about the way God ministered His love through the people, her voice went up a couple of octaves, a glow emanated from her face, and there was such a radiance coming from her spirit.

She spoke about one of my favourite authors of 'Beautiful One' and 'Compelled By Love.' The moment Sarah mentioned Heidi Baker all the memories came flooding back of her selfless acts to go out to abandoned, dying and orphaned children in Africa and other nations who experienced extreme poverty. Sarah said, "Heidi Baker came out of Bethel Church, she was there one evening when I was worshipping, and I just jumped out of my seat, and she gave me a massive hug, she was so lovely and kind, she smiled and laughed and just expressed total joy. I just so love it out there, and I did this healing workshop called Sozo, it was amazing. Basically, I was with two women who just relied on the holy spirit to minister to me, it was really childlike and very liberating. I spent about three hours with them, it was absolutely awesome".

"Wow, I said, God has really done work for you. She also told me of a very blessed singer-songwriter who had ministered in church for some time and was released to go to Bethel Supernatural School of Ministry who now resided in California, Junior Garr. I was feeling a pull in the spirit and God was definitely in this one BIG time. I was like Lord, please order my steps, guide me, direct me, lead me.

That was one conversation that I had the day after my encounter. The other one was with my friend Rachael, who wasn't with me at Miracle Super Sunday, so when she called me, I shared what happened. When I told her about America she literally spurted out through a chuckle that I could be in California.

I thought, "Lord, this is twice in one day that two different people have spoken to me about the same place in America. After we talked, I started to explore Bethel Ministries online so much so that I called them and spoke to a charming lady who broke all protocol. She said I don't usually do this and started to speak into my life and told me I've got a call of leadership on my life and that God will make my journey effortless, that the process will not be complicated, that everything will just run smoothly.

After she finished praying I thanked and blessed her. After the call I smiled and said "over to you God", it's all in your hands. I already had the air miles to go to

California, and I was beginning to see the picture of my destiny etched on the hopes and dreams in my heart.

My new name made me laugh every now and then. My heart was warm, and my future looked bright. Some months later, I'd booked my accommodation, flight, and purchased my conference ticket. That's when the real warfare started, as I went online to do my ESTA, my travelling visa, I was refused entry into the USA. I thought delay does not mean denial!

The prophecy that I got that day became a catalyst for change.

The picture I have painted in regards to the disappointments in the church led me to approach another pastor after the miracle healing super Sunday. She was a lady that I had known at a distance in church. She had a fresh satin complexion and an elegance about her that graced her manner, poise, and charm.

I had approached her in church before, and so she was familiar with the context of some of the things I wanted to work through. She gave me her card that night after service and I discerned that this was going to be the start of what was going to be a truly fantastic journey.

Although I imagined she was in her early fifties her medium frame had carried a youthfulness about her. Her glasses that she wore made her look intellectual like a teacher. She seemed like a nice lady and following this initial encounter, we had briefly spoken outside of church several times before in regards to me seeing her for one to one counselling. At one point I saw her for a health consultation, she was not only a counsellor but a holistic health practitioner as well. We had started to engage in a professional capacity.

Interestingly, the evening that I received my prophecy she was at church with her family, and so I knew that she had further insight into what I had been experiencing and some of the current challenges and coming victories that were on the way. For me, there was a level of expectation that I had from her. I mean she had insight about the child abuse and she knew that I had been dealing with a lot of pain and had seen me struggling to overcome. She was even in a restoration class that I went to once, and also knew based on what was said that I was going through a metamorphosis. From pain to sweet blessings.

It was a bright sunny day in late July, and I found myself crying to my church sister on the phone who so compassionately understood my pain. She had witnessed so many people leave the church because of the way the church had hurt so many of God's children, she was an integral figure in my life when my mother died in 1998. She was one of the first church mothers to come to my aid, but this was to be just the beginning of a special relationship that was going to unfold.

I left church following my mother's death because of the lack of care during my time of bereavement, during this period she was there for me. When I came back to recommit my faith to the Lord in 2008, she was there too. She was in her late fifties early sixties, there was something different about her, I mean apart from her silver hair that adorned her head like a halo, she had the posture and divine elegance of wearing a crown as scribed in the book of Proverbs. Grey hair is a crown of splendour; it is attained by way of righteousness (Prov 16:31).

It wasn't so much her exterior, the clothes or adornment but what she was carrying on the inside.

Man looks on the outside, but God looks at the heart (1st Samuel 16:7).

She was special. If you didn't know Jesus, as a result of meeting her, you came into contact with Him through His humanity. I encountered His peace, and most of all, the love that exuded from her warm, sincere spirit, and there was a level of wisdom that she beheld, I knew she loved God. He was all over her. Her frame reminded me of an oak tree, full-bodied, bountiful and flourishing. Psalms 23, He says that "goodness and mercy shall follow you all the days of your life.

You could see she was carrying this goodness that David spoke about in the bible and I had personally experienced this on such a level that when I was at my weakest, I could taste and see that the Lord was good, through Christ working through her.

I remember when I used to go to her home group in the late nineties with my wounded self literally hanging on to life by the skin of my teeth. For some reason, I was always the last one to leave, and it would just be her and me, and she'd feed me with a hand-picked word. One word that was given to me was from Mathew 5:13 " You are the salt of the earth." I looked at the words and looked at her with a puzzled expression, and without me even uttering a word she began to unfold and break down what the spirit of the Lord was saying.

She said with a soft, comforting voice, " God made you to be a speciality, to add flavour to change the atmosphere and the environment, you are fearfully and wonderfully made." My spirit was taking it in, but my emotions were challenging what she was saying. My feelings were saying I'm hurt, broken and traumatised. My mother had just died, well some months had passed by since her death, but I was still in great pain.

The spirit of rejection was so overwhelming! As a baby Christian, I just couldn't cope with the anguish and I didn't find the church warm, I felt like I didn't belong. The wounding was excruciating.

I had just started doing my Bachelor of Arts at Middlesex University the year before in Race and Culture and Communication studies. This would later be followed by me obtaining my Post Graduate Certificate In Education & Training at Greenwich University and later a Diploma in Counselling skills at London Metropolitan University. The Lord had opened multiple doors for me to become a multi award scholar and sociologist and college lecturer at Southwark College.

In my first year as an undergraduate God had blessed me with a lovely silver Mazda five-door car. God had been good to me, but then, on the other hand, I was experiencing loss, depression, heartache, and abandonment.

So my church mother was the only point of contact I had as a source of comfort. There I was in her house on a Tuesday evening, just me and her at her home in Tottenham being fed the word of God in my spirit, at the same time in a struggle between faith and reality. Those seeds of faith, of God's word, went deep into the depths of me over two decades ago and today I can testify that Jesus' joy has come in the morning. I AM THE SALT OF THE EARTH WITHOUT A SHADOW OF A DOUBT.

Matthew 5:13-16

Salt and Light

13 "You are the salt of the earth. But if the salt loses its saltiness, how can it be made salty again? It is no

longer good for anything, except to be thrown out and trampled underfoot.

14 "You are the light of the world. A town built on a hill cannot be hidden. 15 Neither do people light a lamp and put it under a bowl. Instead they put it on its stand, and it gives light to everyone in the house. 16 In the same way, let your light shine before others, that they may see your good deeds and glorify your Father in heaven.

One of my greatest joys is the many many souls I have brought to the Lord for Christ in recent years, evangelism has become my passion. The most amazing thing about this is I get approached daily, I believe others see His glory revealed in me. There are too many testimonies of salvation and so much more to document here. There is definitely another book just to boast on the goodness of the Lord and marvel at what He has done and is doing in this space.

I said to God in my heart one day, 'You promised that Joy would come in the morning'? I looked heavenward at the blue sky that hung like a canopy over the earth with what looked like clouds hanging like baby mobiles from the sky. I was His child.

Favour Isn't Fair; Signs wonders & Miracles

It's when I think back to me living in Elwood street and after having endured that operation on my feet and survived that agony, I can see how He had His hand on me, even in my early teens. My earliest memories of dancing were when I used to go to the ballet at White Lion Street.

I loved it. The miracle I can testify about now is that several decades later despite the visible scars constantly reminding me of the torture I endured, my feet are Jesus's feet. When I walk you would never know in a million years that I am a survivor of that injustice. All you will experience is an exuberant radiant bright sometimes fluorescent light. He turned my scars into stars. Again, what the devil meant for evil God used it for His good.

Look what else God says about my feet!

Isaiah 52:7 How beautiful upon the mountains Are the feet of him who brings good news, Who proclaims peace, Who brings glad tidings of good things, Who proclaims salvation, Who says to Zion, "Your God reigns!"

I am on the mountain top now! A bearer of GOOD news and proclaiming the peace of the Lord. God is faithful.

Look what else God says about suffering and I can testify to this.

2 Corinthians 4:17

For our light affliction, which is but for a moment, is working for us a far more exceeding and eternal weight of glory.

I have lived the experience of this passage, it's so powerful to engage in His word this way for it to become my reality. When I walk now I am the mobile, living and moving word. His light is a lamp unto my feet and a light unto my path. Psalms 119:105 "Thy word is a lamp unto my feet and a light unto my path".

The Lord came to show me decades later, that my former pastor's family had their house in the same building where I used to dance as a little girl. I remember being at a celebratory service of his service to the body of Christ for twenty-five years and being touched by how God had blessed him.

I didn't think it was a coincidence that I'd be going to White Lion street when I was a young child for lessons in the same building where he preached with his family that resided and had a church there. I believe God predestined this encounter and later joined up the dots for a then colleague to bring me to the Town Hall in Brixton to reconnect with the incredible apostle of my then church.

Also reflecting on my encounter with Corby, my social worker that did her job outside the call of duty, I believe God sent her to me. I mean, she broke all the protocols for working with "Children In Need" like myself. What she invested in me was priceless.

She activated my gift in writing poetry, creativity and the arts. She helped me to find my voice that had been silenced. She treated me as if I was gold when I had been terribly plundered. She always said that I had a lovely voice. She made me feel safe and it was through the light that she shone into my plundered soul that I was able to start using my voice at such a young age.

My headmaster at my primary school used to ask me to sing at assembly on a regular basis and when I got to secondary school I was always asked to lead some of the songs at Christmas carols. By sixteen I was featured in my local paper, the now Islington Tribune, for being a lead singer at some of the local open-air concerts and at the same time began life as a vocalist. The miracle here is the power of encouragement. Corby went over and aboard her call of duty to build me up.

She introduced me to a child therapist who worked with black children, who in turn directed to me Maya Angelo's autobiography and works. It was the first time ever that I read about a black woman being abused but triumphing above it to become a phenomenon. Not only did this empower me to embrace my cultural heritage but it helped me to value myself. Maya Angelou said,

"There is no greater agony than bearing an untold story inside you" - Maya Angelou

Corby related to the unspoken trauma that I was unable to speak about. What she was doing was celebrating me as a black girl of Caribbean heritage and drawing out my beauty from within. It was because of her love that I was able to recover my voice, just as Angelou had become mute because of the abuse, so had I and just as she found liberation, I did too. I love how God used Corby to birth my passion for reading other peoples stories,I was unconsciously learning how to overcome life's challenges by reading narratives of survival, winning in the face of defeat and overcoming impossible situations because of the degree of faith that writers wrote about. It is my hope that in me sharing my testimony that it will strengthen others and impart hope. That giving up is not an option. I pray that my narrative will inspire, empower and bring radical transformation to others.

Back to Corby's interventions for the first time, I learned how to communicate how I felt on paper. This ultimately would lead to me becoming a multi-faceted artist which included me writing poetry, songwriting, singing, broadcasting and so much more.

This autobiography is by far one of my hugest triumphs and while there has been blood sweat and tears there has also been rejoicing, a lifting up and more songs to sing. Who would have ever known that God would have used all the pain to birth in me an obsessive passion to love on the lost and broken to become an

Evangelist, broadcaster and podcaster, worshipper and author to name but some. Doing God's work is a labour of love and brings me priceless joy. After all the bible says, He who wins souls is wise. Proverbs 11:30

Back to how God used Corby, she lavished me with luxury gifts, journals for me to write in, beautiful writing pens, thick embossed colourful paper, adornments, trips out to country cottages to do life story work and just be free. She'd come and take me out to Mcdonalds for lunchtime, pick me up from school and bring me back in time for class. At sixteen she took me to the Savoy Hotel. I truly do believe that her presence made such a life-changing impact on me that to this day I am walking in the transference of a glorious anointing that she imparted to me. This to me has been a life-changing sign and wonder that God sent an angel of light to me through the grace that Corby carried. My life was drastically changed forever as a result of her compassion, kindness, love and selflessness.

I believe in all humility that The Lord has made me a sign and wonder too. Being approached by people wherever I go is a testament to His presence in my life and for that, I am honoured to share His love with all I meet.

Corby lavished so much love and acceptance on me that it created a huge stir in the children's home. She was a sign and wonder. I overheard the then manager of the home talking to one of the care workers saying. I can't believe she's taking her out to all these lavish places, I mean she's just an ordinary child.

Favour is not fair and can cause people to resent you for being treated over and above the norm. God obviously had grand plans for me that were good and not of evil, to prosper me and give me an accepted end (Jeremiah 29:11)

Also the miracle has caused the enemies plots, schemes and plans to be a large footstool. Everything that has tried to destroy me and take me out has served a purpose for me.

I'm reminded of the saying that goes, "what doesn't kill you will make me stronger". Incredibly, He qualifies you to speak to that thing He has delivered you from.

He has called all things to work together for good for me, and nothing has been wasted. While writing this book, I've seen God's hand on my life in a way that I've never seen before. I'm in awe to see him move in the depths of my suffering, anguish, and pain.

I'm reminded of Job in the bible who although lost everything saw God's complete restoration of his life.

The scripture says,

" it was good to be afflicted so I could learn your ways, at the time the pain consumed me but you showed up in my life again and again. I struggled to understand as you fashioned me with your hands, it was good for me to be afflicted, so I could learn your ways".It was good for me to be afflicted so that I might learn your decrees. Psalms 119:79 NIV

The Lord revealed to me while writing my story how much His power has been made perfect in His weakness, I'm in awe.

2 Corinthians 12:8-10

Three times I pleaded with the Lord about this, that it should leave me. But he said to me, "My grace is sufficient for you, for my power is made perfect in weakness." Therefore I will boast all the more gladly of my weaknesses, so that the power of Christ may rest upon me.10 For the sake of Christ, then, I am content with weaknesses, insults, hardships, persecutions, and calamities. For when I am weak, then I am strong.

It's incredible to chronicle, what's happened and scribe my history and see Him in the fire with me. Just like the three Hebrew boys, Shadrach, Meshac, and Abednigo. I'm moved that He loves me so much in a way that my earthly parents never could.

It's a miracle that I can testify today as to what he has done and is doing in my life given the fact that I'm a survivor and victorious.

I'm privileged to be able to reach out to the hurt, broken, and wounded souls to offer them the hope, love, and compassion of Jesus. It is this which fuels my passion for evangelism. I believe that I've got a PhD in life experiences. An intercessor said to me recently you have multiple degrees, I was puzzled. They said, every problem thrown your way God has qualified you, He has ordained you through the afflictions, so that you can be used in a powerful way for His glory. I was humbled listening to this and I thanked God once again for His grace.

God continues to teach me to love my enemies which I cannot do in my own strength, but signs and wonders follow me because I've survived the journey and can testify that it's no longer I that live but Christ who lives in me.

"My old self has been crucified with Christ. It is no longer I who live, but Christ lives in me" (Galatians 2:20 NLT).

Once Again, This Is My Story

"The Spirit of the Lord is upon me because he hath anointed me to preach the gospel to the poor; he hath sent me to heal the brokenhearted, to preach deliverance to the captives, and recovering of sight to the blind, to set at liberty them that are bruised" (Luke 4:18 King James Bible)

"He heals the brokenhearted and binds up their wounds" (Psalms 147:3 New International Version).

There really is so much revelation and power that comes from writing. The grace that I've got from telling my story is that the Lord has birthed my ministry, it's as if the light bulb has come on. It makes sense now, the process, the journey, the walk to freedom!

How can you reach out to someone if you have been through nothing? He has qualified me to reach out to the orphans, rejected children in emotional anguish and the forgotten ones. The misfits and others who are marginalised, the exceptional ones who don't realise that the reason they don't fit in is that they're outstanding, that is, standing outside so that they can shine BRIGHTER.

Another miracle that happened is that He qualified me to identify the signs and symptoms of abuse by training me to be a lecturer in Childcare and Health and Social care to show practitioners how to protect children. The testimony here is that Christ is a curse breaker, I've been able to promote safeguarding rather than become a perpetrator.

How did I become an encourager, singer, psalmist, songwriter, poet, social worker, multi-award-winning scholar, sociologist, lecturer, trainer, mentor, life coach, certified reader, talk for health chair, laughter therapist, voice model, broadcaster, orator, author, missionary, humanitarian and philanthropist and evangelist? How did I develop a burden and be called to mother hurting children that have been deprived, abandoned and rejected in orphanages?

God did it!

The song Blessed Assurance written by Fanny Crosby resounds in my spirit here.
Blessed assurance, Jesus is mine!
Oh, what a foretaste of glory divine!
Heir of salvation, purchase of God,
Born of His Spirit, washed in His blood.

    Refrain:
    This is my story, this is my song,
    Praising my Savior all the day long;
    This is my story, this is my song,
    Praising my Savior all the day long.

Perfect submission, perfect delight,

Visions of rapture now burst on my sight;

Angels, descending, bring from above

Echoes of mercy, whispers of love.

Perfect submission, all is at rest,

I in my Savior am happy and blest,

Watching and waiting, looking above,

Filled with His goodness, lost in His love.

He equipped me with a degree in Sociology, obtaining a BA Hons In Race and Culture and Communication Studies in 2000, and then doing my Teacher Training at Greenwich University where I had an incredible time with the most amazing students and fantastic lecturer, then obtaining my Diploma In Counselling Skills, It was so He could be glorified.

Oh, I've skipped the part where he sent me to work in places like Barnardos, a family centre for children who were at risk and on the child protection register. These were the children like baby P, Jamie Bulger, and Victoria Climbe. If you're not familiar with these names their children that were abused and on the child protection register who devastatingly lost their precious lives at the hands of their perpetrators.

As a sociologist, He has trained me to deliver programs in child health and a whole range of other modules in further education to young people and adults. But the real essence of the fantastic triumph here is that what happened to me when I was a child, what I had to go through and survive stopped with me, the pattern and cycle has been interrupted. The saying hurt people, hurt people has not been the case for me. I made a decision and with the help of God Almighty to rise above this. It really is a choice. I continue to ask God to help such people to deliver them from their weakness that perpetuates abusive patterns. I am a living witness that God is able to break off toxic soul ties.

Freedom has come from not perpetuating negative generational patterns. Jesus "breaks every chain," glory to God. He is a curse for you and me so that we could be set free and delivered from the power of satan.

Sometimes I think favour isn't fair because God will cause you to stand out from the crowd, sometimes that can include your own family, well for me it was

. I remember when I was in my early twenties, by this time I'd completed my two years of studies in college, had passed my driving test at eighteen and was taking home a salary as a support worker, working with vulnerable children. Someone who I'd regarded as a close relative said to me, " leave the country and go abroad". I had mixed feelings when I heard this. I felt like I was a misfit, the odd one out.

Just as Jesus was rejected by men, despised and had many enemies, I felt that way at his stage in my life in my own biological family. I was different in many ways, people said they liked the way I spoke, I was the first in my generation to work from an early age, pass my driving test at a young age, excel in higher education and become professionally trained as a lecturer, mentor and coach with my own company under my birth name that provided coaching and training. I came to appreciate through a lot of rejection by others that God was calling me to be the "chief cornerstone." (Psalms 118:22)

Also, the favour of God is so amazing because I don't look like where I've come from, given the severity of the abuse that was inflicted on me. God has enabled me to triumph through the many trials with my head held high because my eyes have been set on Him.

I'm reminded of a song that we used to sing at church in the mid-90s that says " I will lift up my eyes to the hills, from where cometh my help, my help cometh from the Lord which make heaven and earth."I never imagined that I'd get to the age I am now in one piece coupled with so much resentment by the very people I thought would have "celebrated" my survival.

As an overcomer coming out with the victory, God has equipped me with many gifts, talents, and abilities which I humbly appreciate.

In Matthew 10:34-36 Jesus said He had come at this time not to bring peace to the earth, but a sword, a weapon which divides and severs. As a result of His visit to earth, some children would be set against parents, and a man's enemies might be those within his own household. This is because many who choose to follow Christ are hated by their family members. This may be part of the cost of discipleship, for love of family should not be greater than love for the Lord.

True followers of Christ must be willing to give up, even to the point of "hating" all that is in our lives, even our own families, if we are to be worthy of Him (Mathew 10:37-39). In so doing, we find our lives in return for having given them up to Jesus Christ.

He has given me inner strength and resilience that comes from His spirit.

I choose to believe God's word only concerning who I am in Him and loving who He created me to be. After many years yearning to be loved, appreciated and accepted by my natural family I came to value that being the odd one out like Joseph is a blessing. His assignment was to bless them, and so is mine.

God set it up in 2009 for me to be mentored by a highly regarded bishop as my business coach. We had several one to one sessions over a few months, and I have to say this quality time of impartation was nothing short of amazing. There really is power in prophecy.

Bishop would tell me that I was going to be a chief executive officer of my own company which manifested. He said that I would be empowered by having my own corporation, which I did, and he spoke some awesome things into my destiny and purpose which is coming to pass. I am blessed.

I am inspired from this poem by Marianne Williamsom and I hope it inspires you too,

"Our deepest fear is not that we are inadequate. Our deepest fear is that we are powerful beyond measure.

It is our light, not our darkness that most frightens us. We ask ourselves, who am I to be brilliant, gorgeous, talented, fabulous? Actually, who are you not to be? You are a child of God. Your playing small does not serve the world. There is nothing enlightened about shrinking so that other people won't feel insecure around you. We are all meant to shine as children do. We were born to make manifest the glory of God that is within us. It's not just in some of us; it's in everyone. And as we let our own light shine we unconsciously give other people permission to do the same. As we are liberated from our own fear, our presence automatically liberates others".

I share this to encourage you as it helped me that greatness is birthed through affliction and the story of Nelson Mandela often encouraged me during my journey as a survivor. His captivity in Robin Island for twenty-seven years showed me that your tomb, the thing that imprisoned you can become your womb for birthing brilliance and amazing things. After all, This book has come out of that place. Mandela, when freed embraced His captors with love. I too am freed through forgiveness.

I pray that as you have read my story that God revealed to you in some way, shape, or form that He is a loving, faithful and merciful God. Yes, the process can be horrific, debilitating at times I have felt at times that the wind has been taken beneath my sails, but to God be the glory, the same power that raised Lazurus from the dead is active, alive and working in me. Thanks are to Jesus, the saviour of my soul.

As a victor, sometimes the enemy tries to demote who you are, because He was chucked out of heaven he tries to bring you down to his low level by feeling easily intimidated, withdrawn, fearful and having weak confidence and low self-esteem. God has lifted up my head, He said be lifted up ye everlasting doors and the king of glory shall come in. Psalms 24:7-10

I wanted to share this with you to encourage you that God qualifies the unqualified and uses the foolish things of the world to confound the wise. God can use anyone, and that includes you and I.

Noah was a drunk, Abraham was too old, Jacob was a liar, Leah was ugly, Joseph was abused, Moses had a stuttering problem, Gideon was afraid, Sampson had long hair and was a womanizer, Rahab was a prostitute, Jerimiah and Timothy were too young, David had an affair with a murderer, Elijah was suicidal, Isaiah was suicidal, Jonah ran from God, Naomi was a widow, Job went bankrupt, Peter denied Christ, The disciples fell asleep while praying, the samaritan woman was divorced, Zaccheus was too small, Paul was too religious, Timothy had an ulcer, Lazarus was dead.

DESIDERATA

I'm reminded of God speaking to me long before I ever did the sinner's prayer. We were talking over twenty-odd years ago when a friend and I had gone along to a cultural event in west London. Selina had invited me to this venue on the other side of London, and it was here that I was drawn to a piece of writing that spoke to me so powerfully that I had to buy it.

Looking back decades later, I realize that God was with me in the wilderness. This writing was called DESIDERATA that I had kept as a continuous reminder of His love for me even when I didn't know Him. It guided me to quiet times of peace and reflection in what I was experiencing in a troubled world. Without me realizing it God was guiding me to keep my peace and be humble, and I would even go as far to say that even though it wasn't precisely the ten commandments, it gave me some Godly morals to abide by.

Years later I came to learn a song called 'It Is Well With My Soul', a beautiful melodic worship song whereupon listening to it and even singing it the Lord would minister His wonderful grace. I just think it is so amazing to look back on the forty plus decades of my life and see that God dropped golden nuggets, stars and diamonds and precious pearls that manifested themselves in precious souls, angels amongst strangers, poems like the one you're about to read and special moments infused with His love, mercy, grace, and passion.

Experiences that touched my spirit and revived my weary soul like listening to and falling in love with Lavine Hudson, a fantastic gospel singer that I used to listen to way before I got saved. I played her records almost every day during a season of my life, not realizing that God was using the gospel to penetrate my heart with His amazing grace.

This is Desiderata.

"GO PLACIDLY AMID THE NOISE & HASTE & REMEMBER WHAT PEACE THERE MAY BE IN silence. As far as possible, be on good terms with all persons. Speak your truth quietly and clearly, even the dull and ignorant; they too have their story. * Avoid loud and aggressive persons, they are vexations to the spirit. If you compare yourselves to others, you may become vain and bitter; for there will always be greater and lesser persons than yourself. Enjoy your achievements as well as your plans.*Keep interested in your career, however humble; it is a real possession in the changing fortunes of time. Exercise cautions in your affairs; for the world is full trickery. But let this not blind you to what virtue there is; many persons strive for high ideals, and everywhere life is whole of heroism. * Be yourself, Especially, do not feign affection. Neither be cynical about love, in the face of aridity and disenchantment it is a perennial as the grass. * Take kindly to the counsel of the years, gracefully surrendering the things of youth. Nurture strength of spirit to shield you in sudden misfortune But do not distress yourself with imaginings. Many fears are born of fatigue and loneliness. Beyond a wholesome discipline, be gentle with yourself. * You are a child of the universe, no less than the trees or the stars; you have a right to be here. And whether or not it is clear to you, no doubt the universe is unfolding as it should. * Therefore be at peace with God whatever you conceive Him to be and whatever your labour and aspirations, in the noisy confusions of life keep peace with your soul. With all its sham, drudgery, and broken dreams, it is a beautiful world. Be careful, Strive to be happy**

FOUND IN OLD STREET. ST. PAULS CHURCH, BALTIMORE, DATED 1692

Every Glory Has A Story

As I conclude my story, I really feel I need to share how I have come to appreciate all the experiences that I have had, particularly the painful ones. It has built my character, deepened my humility, has equipped me with extraordinary compassion and I have been given a voice that God Himself has blessed. He has empowered me through the pain and I have found freedom in him as I mount up on wings as an eagle. Isaiah 40:31

The painful times have gifted me with the grace that causes strangers to approach me and enquire as to who I am and where I am from. What a beautiful way for me to testify about the Lord Jesus Christ.

With far too many to name, I have led multitudes of people to the Lord, winning souls with others and going about my daily affairs and connecting with people where they are at and sharing The Love of God with them in a way that they can encounter Jesus.

Maybe I should write a book just for those testimonies where many people have received salvation. The joy is exhilarating.

Growing up and even as an adult, there were times when I just couldn't get my head around the gravity of what I was enduring. It just didn't make sense. When I am having a moment, if I'm honest, sometimes I still question God, but when I look back over my life and see how He has miraculously strengthened and sustained me I am so so encouraged.

The scripture says though, "that though I walk through the valley of the shadow of death, I shall fear no evil", (Psalms 23:4).

During the testing times, I would ask how could God really love me when I had no sense of belonging and was confronted with such deprivation of not growing up in a loving family.

Why was life so cruel? There were so many questions that would sometimes spin around my mind that at times, I just wanted to escape this cruel, dark, cold world.

Thank God I didn't totally give up and that my life has been preserved to experience the joy of carrying His presence that so often captivates others and ushers them in to have an encounter with His spirit that is in me. Indeed, greater is He that is in me than He that is in the world! (John 4:4). Also, as it was with Esther in the bible, so it is with me. For you have come to the kingdom for such a time as this (Esther 4:14).

Not too long ago, I was sharing the love of God with a small outreach group. The son (sun) was so glorious that day. As we gathered and prayed literally just after we said amen to the prayer something came over me almost instantaneously. A boldness, a fearlessness, I became bright, expansive and bursting with the power of God's love.

I began sharing to people around me how much God loved them, some were so captivated by my passionate conviction that I began to testify what God had done for me. That I was a reject, an orphan that was treated so cruel and violated to the core that some began to cry.

When I saw them weep, I told them how much God loved them. That the same God that has been with me through thick and thin is the same God that wants to be with them, come into their hearts so that He could be their Lord and saviour. On one outreach with a team of evangelists and after only one and a half hours twenty-two people came to the Lord.

I experience great power through winning souls, a glorious, captivating, and animated presence in the Holy Spirit. I experience something so profound. Witnessing God's love for the lost is so healing for me. Rescuing the perishing is cathartic, it's a love zone where there's no judgment by testifying to the lost and walking in the power and anointing of God. It's as if I get to boast about The Lord by sharing my story and showing them that I am a living miracle.

Looking into the eyes of a soul in pain and despair and building a strong rapport with others brings me so much meaning, hope, and strength to me. I experienced the power like that of Billy Graham, Kathryn Kulman and Reinhard Hart Bonke and Jerry Eze and so many others who find their strength in God and are anointed to fulfill their purpose.

By sharing my story God has ministered great relief to me. So much of what tried to annihilate me in my former years made no sense. The breaking of me was the making of me. I am like, OK, Lord, so this is what you mean when you said that my suffering would produce a greater Glory.

For our light affliction, which is but for a moment, worketh for us a far more exceeding and eternal weight of glory. 2 Corinthians 4:17 KJV

All of a sudden what God had spoken to me all these years, the words burst open. I have overcome by testifying. And they overcame by the blood of the Lamb and by the word of their testimony, and they loved not their lives unto death. Revelation 12:11

Another scripture that became my reality, particularly when evangelising
was in regards to the uncontainable joy that weeping would endure for a night, but that joy would come in the morning (Psalms 30:5), and that the pleasure of the Lord is my strength (Nehemiah 8:10).

The Holy Spirit told me that despite my childhood sometimes feeling so agonising that He was using everything I had been through, good, bad and ugly which I experienced really profoundly. I found that out in the field evangelising with the team that I was pulled to connecting with all the outcasts, rejects, alcoholics, neglected children and adults and all those precious souls that society had given up on.

Finally, it made sense! I could relate to these special people because I had lived experience of what they were going through. I could relate to their abuse, pain, emptiness, fear, rejection, and abandonment. God was using my past to fulfil my calling to win the lost. I LOVE IT. More so because these souls loved God in me and I too could see Christ in them.

They accepted my truth, loved my authenticity, that I wasn't putting on the pretence of being a perfect Christian. These people honoured God's Love for me, and I loved and still do love the fact that I can bare my soul to the hurting, that my scars have become stars and I am loved as an overcomer.

I've been readily and warmly embraced when witnessing His love, it has been the ultimate epiphany of unconditional positive regard. A place where I experience true belonging. A judgement-free space of acceptance and honour. Something that I battled with for many, many years.

I am in my element when winning souls for Christ. It's an unspeakable labour of love and freedom. The really fantastic thing here too is that my passion, purpose, and values are aligned to the will of my heavenly Father.

"All things work together for good for them that love the Lord" (Romans 8:28).

It's one thing reading scripture and believing it by faith but a totally different experience when for me when I am looking into the eyes of someone who's tired of holding on, seeing the loneliness, pain, despair, abandonment, and anguish in their soul and being able to encourage them to see the Lord bring hope and comfort. Then using my lived experience being used as a key to release them with the promise of the gospel and watch pain change to love and joy. This is the most priceless experience ever for so many reasons.

The spirit of the Lord is upon me because the Lord has anointed me to proclaim good news to the poor. He has sent me to bind up the brokenhearted, to proclaim freedom for the captives and release from darkness for the prisoners. God gave me his authoritative scripture some years ago, and I have always loved reading it, but I've gone from reading it to experiencing this as my reality, and I am truly humbled (Isaiah 61:1).

When I first started writing this story in 2013, the same year when I was sinking into such a deep depression, still at my old church and through what appeared to be a close covenant relationship with my then prayer partner/ church mother. I had no idea of the attack on my life that was about to be unleashed. Sometimes, it's tough to comprehend, but God says to me that His ways are not my ways and that I should not lean unto my own understanding (Proverbs 3:5) Quite challenging!

Without God's grace to withstand such an assault on my life to release up till now my untold story, I think it would have been totally impossible to have survived. Maybe if I had the wisdom that I have now, I might not have allowed myself to be open to revisiting infant and childhood trauma, pain and torture in the church environment. I came to realise that this was not a safe place to revisit the historical pain as there were no trained people there to help me to heal and recover well.

I may not have been so naive and laid myself so open and vulnerable to experiencing such excruciating childhood memories and pain that had been buried for decades. The process wreaked havoc on my health which impacted my entire life.

Writing this led me to experience such agony, similar to what Job experienced in the bible. Reliving the torturous early memories I endured impacted my physical body in such a way that as we speak I am constantly decreeing and declaring healing over my entire body, mind, spirit, and soul. Truth be told, having been on flight for over thirty-five years and highly functioning, God has seen fit for me to experience this Gethsamanee to experience deep healing first for myself then bring this to others.

There were not only birthing pangs, but the labour of this book bought much anguish by relieving so much childhood trauma. If I could have changed the way the story was birthed out, I think I would have allowed it to happen through a therapeutic relationship that would have been much more safe and gentle. Nevertheless, I have miraculously survived and continue to fight from victory which was guaranteed at Golgotha on the cross on Calvary.

The critical thing in this process has been about using what was meant to destroy me as a means to testify of God's amazing grace and in doing so emptying hell of the perishing and filling heaven with precious souls. It's about serving others. There really is great power in sharing your story. I am reminded of a quote that says, " you can recognize survivors of abuse by their courage. When silence is so very inviting, they step forward and share their truth, so others know they are not alone".

Forgiveness really is the antidote to pain, and I humbly say it is a work in progress, I have had to forgive myself too for allowing the mistreatment that I endured from my primary caregivers to become my reality by believing the lie that I was unlovable, a reject and unworthy. I had to repent of agreeing with the opposite of what God spoke over my life.

I grew up covered in shame and condemnation. I didn't know any other way. Now decades later, the healing really is accepting that God has released me from all shame. His love for me is from everlasting to everlasting. I can finally agree with God that I am fearfully and wonderfully and marvellously made (Psalms 139:9) and that I am the apple of His eye (Psalms 17:8).

Recently I was on an inspirational course, in fact, I spent the weekend with some incredible people acquiring some tools that I could use in my role as a Laughter Therapist at a children's school in an amazing hospital. I was learning how to facilitate happiness, it actually felt like I was learning to play again, it was so much fun. Literally, I spent the whole weekend laughing.

On the second day, we did an exercise called capes of kindness. Basically, in the vein of spreading compassion, care, and love, each of us was able to write anonymous comments about how we perceived each other. I was in awe to read so many touching things that people had written about me. Things like, I feel that I have met my soulmate, I love your positivity, your bubbly, what an awesome lady you are! Thank you for lighting up the room, people warm to you like sunshine and so on and so on.

Every glory has a story. Hearing this type of feedback is deeply gratifying, then I think if only they knew half the price I had to pay to stay alive. Then the spirit in me kicks in, and I believe, yes, God you're being glorified and lifted up. Your presence is drawing people to you. I mean, how amazing is that? That I get to show off the Holy Spirit who is so radiant and bright. Go God!

I remember being on a wellbeing training course some time ago, it lasted over several weekends. Again I had the opportunity to learn and apply some communicative skills which included empathic listening. I loved it, we were a relatively large diverse group that bonded really well.

On the last day, we were allowed to share something special that was meaningful to us, something that had personal value. Well, I shared a poem called "Covered" that I had written the previous night that read like this:

Every hurdle I surpassed
Was a stepping stone into genius
Awe wonder gifts and talents

Were birthed out of tragedy

18 life crises

Including being orphaned

& defeating death

That tried to rob me

But it couldn't take my last breath

Rejection

Abandonment

Stigma and shame

Tried to shackle me in the children's

home and to this day
I nurse the pain

You see bright colours

resembling paradise

But to me I wear plasters

So I don't bleed on the outside

The trials of life

Have birthed my many gifts

I discovered my genius

At the bottom of the pit

From the age of innocence

I learned to sing

To write songs and poems

That bough deep inner healing

The deeper the pain

The deeper the love

And as I rise from the ashes

I glide above life's storms to seek

Shalom and bring light

And mercy

And the peace of a dove

By the time I looked up, I heard sobs and witnessed

the silent shedding of tears. Each person was given a

minute to write a letter of appreciation, after having

poured out their hearts of gratitude, each leaving their seats in the large circle we were sitting in, to come and place their written sentiments in my lap.

I too wept tears of love and gratitude. I got seventeen handwritten letters altogether. Every glory does indeed have a story. What I mean is that for everything I had suffered God somehow and in His own miraculous way used it to become some kind of gift, a ray of hope, a chance to be a light in the dark, to share a testimony, an encouragement to someone that after all no pain is wasted.

Some of the letters wrote like this:

"I am so moved. Who would ever know? It shouldn't surprise me that you've been through all that because I know that the people who shine brightest are the ones who have been through the valley of the shadow of death .... I am amazed by you, your brightness and resilience after everything. Thank you so much for being here, for being such a treasure". Signed Nicky

"The eloquent life force, and poet with words and colours, I hope you become a permanent member of the community and look forward to knowing you and having more of your beautiful poems". Signed Roy

"What to say? Where to start? You are just precious, as your poem rightly says. I admire your courage and your bright colours. They are not plasters to me, they are a sign of a heart full of wisdom and dignity. I enjoyed being with you in this group and will always treasure every word we shared. Keep it is, keep it strong, with love". Signed Therese

"I am struggling to find words to match your fantastic poem. You are a wonderful person. I imagine it must have been tough to go through some of the experiences you share with us. But I appreciate your inspirational capability to turn your vulnerability into strengths. Thank you for being part of this group. You empowered me". Signed Nivran

"Wow. You're fabulous. Wish we could bottle you up and drink you daily. I loved your poem, which touched me deeply especially when you described the outfits as plasters. I hope can feel one day without these outfits and in your birthday suit as wonderful a person as I and many here feel you be. Thank you, XXX". Signed Rachael

"Ray of the beautiful light that brightens this room. Your amazing combination of strength and vulnerability blows me away! Your kind words and generosity of spirit to others (I'll never forget you calling me Brene Brown!!) Your lyricism, not just in your incredible poem, but in the depth and beauty of every word you say. You are a real beauty". XX Chiara

"I appreciate your resilience, your strength, and courage. Your bright smile and kind heart. You are a radiating person, and I wish to get to know you better and one day call you friend. I am thankful for you to have come to this course and for sharing and being fully engaged. Thank you for being you. Hugs and best wishes". Sophie

"When you walked into the room, you got my attention straight away. Strong character, outgoing, bubbly, joyful person. This is how I see you, so live in the moment that is now. Because we have already been through the worst". Dean X

To this day, I have a special bright yellow envelope where I keep all these handwritten words of affirmations that are a stark reminder of His amazing grace.

The Lord has invested so much in me, and I am forever grateful that He has miraculously preserved my life. It's because of Him that I started writing at the age of eleven, firstly with poetry, then songwriting and then co-producing some of my material. It was through developing a love of literature of all kinds and then becoming addicted to the word of God that has led me on my journey of encouraging others. I am commanded to shine as are you and when you yield to the promises of God, He hastens to perform His word. I pray that the Lord has encouraged you, blessed you, strengthened and edified you while reading my story. He loves you with an everlasting love and gave His only begotten son so that you would not die but have everlasting and eternal life. (John 3:16).

My story was also written to bring people out of darkness into redemption. It's my prayer for you that you would have experienced God for yourself as you have read my narrative, maybe you have even given your heart to the Lord by reciting the sinner prayer from your heart.

At times during writing, this book the presence of God was so strong. It was a profound awareness of His power, His strength, His invisible mighty hand that reached down and rescued me from the trenches of what looked like a hopeless situation.

As I am writing this at 4 AM in the morning in the winter, it's pre-dawn, I'm sitting in my snug watching the flickering flame of a candle and I'm aware of His Presence again. His peace that transcends all understanding.

I'm reminded of the poem about God's footprints in the sand and for me a powerful epiphany that only God could have been with and carried me through some of the most agonising times of my life. I truly believe that

God has carried me all the way through my life and He continues to do so, as you read these words from Footprints in the sand be encouraged that this is my reality. Maybe it can become yours too?

One night I dreamed a dream.
As I was walking along the beach with my Lord.
Across the dark sky flashed scenes from my life.
For each scene, I noticed two sets of footprints in the sand,
One belonging to me and one to my Lord.
After the last scene of my life flashed before me,
I looked back at the footprints in the sand.
I noticed that at many times along the path of my life,
especially at the very lowest and saddest times,
there was only one set of footprints.
This really troubled me, so I asked the Lord about it.
"Lord, you said once I decided to follow you,
You'd walk with me all the way.

But I noticed that during the saddest and most troublesome times of my life,

there was only one set of footprints.

I don't understand why, when I needed You the most, You would leave me."

He whispered, "My precious child, I love you and will never leave you

Never, ever, during your trials and testings.

When you saw only one set of footprints,

It was then that I carried you."

I know for sure that these trials have worked for my good because through them I have been gifted a multitude of treasures. It's the profound empathy I have for the overlooked and castaways that society has ignored. It's the rejected ones that have been abandoned that I am moved to encourage.

It's the lost souls that I'm deeply moved to share my testimony with to give hope to the hopeless and to let them see how real the God of my suffering has been.

Who would have known that in 2019 alone more than eighty souls have come to the Lord through my testimony? Who would have known that I would be headhunted by pastors to sow into my anointing by asking me to come and Evangelise with them because they recognised the grace on my life to win souls?

Who would have known that God would hand-pick some special people to sponsor my life narrative through writing this book because they too saw the hand of God on my life? I am so very grateful for those precious souls for their unwavering support. GOD BLESS YOU.

Who would have known that my destiny and purpose and calling would have been birthed out of such devastation and ashes? I would never have thought that the past agony was the catalyst to birth a haven in my spirit for precious souls.

Through the pain, God created a sanctuary within, a place of love, hope and belonging for the oppressed, overlooked and abandoned to be supported and loved on. Who would have known that God would have used all my experiences, good, bad and otherwise, to build my character and birth my call to ministry to neglected children?

Because God has favoured me (Luke 1:28) through me initially being moved by the plight of precious souls in need of support, connection and encouragement. Only God could have equipped me to minister to such people through the intense pain I have experienced which was God's way of giving me heartfelt compassion for my heart to beat for the things that concern him.

One day I will be at the orphanage which is in my spirit and is a physical holding space for the abused, hurt and forgotten. This fills my heart with so much joy. It's my calling, my purpose and destiny to love abandoned children and minister the deep love of God to them.

Miraculously, God has laid on the heart of others to ask me to come and minister at various churches to share my passion to worship, sing and share my story. What an honour for God to use me in this way to share the love of The Father.

The Lord Himself has comforted and empowered me with these precious passages:

Romans 8:18

For I consider that the sufferings of this present time are not worthy to be compared with the glory which shall be revealed in us.

Who would have known that God would cause the intense suffering I endured to produce a thick substance of divine joy in and through my spirit

Proverbs 11:30

The fruit of the righteous is a tree of life, And he who wins souls is wise.

How amazing it is though that through it all God has indeed all things to work together? My utmost passion at this time in my life is to win souls, souls, souls. I LOVE IT.

.Mathew 6:19-21

Do not store up for yourselves treasures on earth, where moths and vermin destroy, and where thieves break in and steal. 20 But store up for yourselves treasures in heaven, where moths and vermin do not destroy, and where thieves do not break in and steal. 21 For where your treasure is, there your heart will be also.

Romans 8:18

For I consider that the sufferings of this present time are not worthy to be compared with the glory which shall be revealed in us.

If you feel led I invite you to receive the gift Jesus in your heart by saying the sinner's prayer below. He has given me the priceless gift of eternal life, I mean, how amazing is that! He is knocking gently on the door of your heart, will you let Him in.

The Sinner's Prayer

The sinner's prayer must come from your heart, and we hope this will help you to invite Jesus into yours. This prayer is here only as a guide. We urge you to pour out your heart to Jesus in your own words.

"Heavenly Father, have mercy on me, a sinner. I believe in you and that your word is true. I believe that Jesus Christ is the Son of the living God and that he died on the cross so that I may now have forgiveness for my sins and eternal life. I know that without you in my heart, my life is meaningless.

I believe in my heart that you, Lord God, raised Him from the dead. Please, Jesus, forgive me, for every sin I have ever committed or done in my heart, please Lord Jesus, forgive me and come into my heart as my personal Lord and Savior today. I need you to be my Father and my friend.

I give you my life and ask you to take full control from this moment on; I pray this in the name of Jesus Christ."

Amen.

If you said this prayer sincerely from your heart, congratulations. Heaven rejoices over one. You are now a beloved child of the most high God. I pray that you will ask the LORD to show you a Bible Believing Church where you will be loved and nurtured amongst the brethren of Christ who first loved us.

I pray that sharing my story has been a blessing to you, I thank you for taking the time to read my narrative and maybe share it with someone else who will be encouraged too. Now, I am focused more than ever and with a burden to go and mother my children that I have yet to love on in the natural world at my God-ordained orphanage. THE VISION IS COMPELLING AND IS COMING TO PASS

Just one last song by Kari Jobe

Healer / Kari Jobe

You hold my very moment

You calm my raging seas

You walk with me through fire

And heal all my disease

I trust in You, I trust in You

I believe You're my healer

I believe You are all I need

I believe

And I believe You're my portion

I believe You're more than enough for me

Jesus You're all I need

318

You hold my very moment

You calm my raging seas

You walk with me through fire

And heal all my disease

I trust in You, Lord I trust in You

I believe You're my healer

I believe You are all I need

Oh, I believe

I believe You're my portion

I believe You're more than enough for me

Jesus You're all I need

Nothing is impossible for You

Nothing is impossible

Nothing is impossible for You

You hold my world in Your hands

Songwriters: Lois Irwi

As I finally close I just want to say two things.

Why so many feathers around me in the last days of writing my story? Well, God took me to Psalms 91 which says in verse 4, "He will cover you with his feather, and under His wings you will find refuge, his faithfulness will be your shield and rampart".

I am totally overwhelmed by such a beautiful passage as I engage with the reality of His divine covering and most overpowering love.

Lastly,

Today I am blessed with the reality of experiencing healing and being a source of healing to others. My voice has been preserved to be His mouthpiece in the earth and for that, I have no words but am humbled by the unending love of Abba Father

I am sending you love. I hope that as you have listened to my story that you realise that you have read one of the most beautiful love stories ever. A love that I encountered when I gave my heart To The Lord My Saviour. It's through this love that I am divorced from the pain of my story and embody the anointing to testify about the greatness of God. My assignment is to teach what I know about overcoming, releasing and forgiving through sharing life lessons from the pain to help you in your journey too. To the abused, abandoned, rejected, despised, forgotten and mistreated, stigmatised and lonely. To the overlooked and hurting, may you experience the love I am filled and flooded with through the supernatural touch of Abba Father. May the love that overwhelms me with euphoric joy be your reality too. May you be transformed into the most adorable loving radiant and blissful soul. You are so loved. Believe that.

With Love, Candy

Resources

Child Abuse Resources

Thirtyone:eight - 0303 003 11 11 9am to 5pm Monday - Friday Office Hours (Outside these hours Emergency only)

Childline - children can phone 0800 1111 for free

Action for Children - (for children and adults)

NSPCC - for Adults concerned about a child, free phone (24 hour)0800 808 5000

Domestic Abuse Resources

Womens Aid https://www.womensaid.org.uk/

Jewish Womens Aid https://www.jwa.org.uk/

National Domestic Abuse

https://www.nationaldahelpline.org.uk/ Freephone 0808
2000 247

Rape Support Resources

Rape Crisis Centres

England: 020 78371600

Scotland: 0141 221 8448

Wales: 01222 733 929

Rape Crisis Federation

Dissociation

Dissociation in the UK - Information on the subject, and
help finding a qualified therapist.

General

UCB Prayerline

Premier Lifeline National Christian Helpline

Nafsiyat InterCultural Therapy Centre

Womens Therapy Centres - Advice and information phone no: 020 7263 6200

Monday to Friday 10am-12pm; 2pm-4pm; thursday 6pm-8pm

Male Survivors - phone no:020 7833 3737

Tuesday, Wednesday, and Thursday 7pm-10pm

The Samaritans - 24 hour listening,

Self Harm

Harmless- https://harmless.org.uk/

Heads Above the Waves- https://hatw.co.uk/

Mental Health and Wellbeing

Careline - Telephone: 020 8514 1177

Helpline and counselling for children, young people and adults, on ANY issue of concern.

Open Mon-Fri 10am-4pm AND 7pm-10pm.

No Panic - Freephone 0808 808 0545 — 10am-10pm daily.

Support for those suffering from panic attacks, phobias, obsessive compulsive disorders, and other anxiety related disorders.

British Association for Counselling - phone no: 01788 578328 or send S.A.E. for information to: BAC, 1 Regent Place, Rugby, CV21 2JP

<u>Mind</u> - phone no: 020 85192122

<u>Relate</u> - Offers counselling, can help with relational difficulties and sexual problems,

Victim support - Phone no: 020 7735 9166

The National Eating Disorders Association - Lots of information and help on all aspects of eating disorders including Anorexia Nervosa, Bulimia Nervosa, Binge Eating Disorder, and related eating disorders.

Helplines 01603 621414 (open 9:00 to 18:30 weekdays)

Youthline 01603 765050 (open 16:00 to 18:00 weekdays)

Health

<u>NHS 111</u> England

<u>UK Health</u> -Hundreds of pages of information and resources covering healthy eating, mental health, addiction and abuse.

Printed in Great Britain
by Amazon

83747904R00188